The Most Feared And Powerful Pharaohs Of Ancient Egypt

Rulers That Shaped The Egyptian Empire Into One Of The Most Famous Civilizations In History

James C. Hockley

Table of Contents

Introduction

Exploring the millennia-rich history of Ancient Egypt is like taking a walk through an abyss of truths and mysteries. Over the years, archeologists, scientists, and experts in different fields have continued to reveal and popularize the beautifully interlinked stories of the Ancient Egyptian civilization, what it meant for those who lived during that time, and also what it means for the people of the modern world. Those who lived in the predynastic Nile Valley and Nile Delta cultures and the Dynastic periods of the Ancient Egyptian civilization took nothing for granted and ascribed special meanings to nature as much as they did their own inventions. Natural events such as the yearly flooding of the Nile inspired their conception of time and the ancient Egyptian calendar to which the Gregorian calendar used in the West today can be traced. In this regard, it has been said that "the West has long been fascinated by the East. The former's music, art, literature, and architecture are peppered with learned and romanticized interpretations of the latter" (Marshall Cavendish Corporation, 2011, p. 4).

For more than 3,000 years, nearly 200 pharaohs emerged from multiple dynasties to shape and color the story of Ancient Egypt in ways that made the civilization the envy of its contemporaries. Despite the interruptions of the Intermediate Periods—often described by some as crisis periods, and "dark periods" or "dark ages" by the more sardonic scholars and people with some interest in Egyptology—the challenges, crises, and advancements of those ancient days were the hallmark of a civilization moving unwaveringly forward. Whether it was the little steps of the predynastic millenniums (6000 B.C.E.-3150 B.C.E) that produced "metal items, woven baskets, tanned animal hides, hunting tools and woven fabrics" (Holmes, 2011), or the giant leap from being a vast territory of divided tribes to a territory of a united population brought about by King Menes or Narmer at the start of the Early Dynastic Period (ca. 3150 B.C.E.), there is a lot more to credit Ancient Egypt for than there is not.

To give meaning to the sun, the earth, the sky, and natural phenomena in general, kings were seen as divine beings, and the Egyptians attached one divine power or another to hundreds of gods and goddesses, including the omnipotent Atum, the god of wisdom Thoth, and the ruler of the Land of the Dead, Osiris. In addition to their religious beliefs and pioneering thoughts in theology was the magic created in buildings and structures made with stones and rocks, the making of the sarcophagus or complexly decorated stone coffin, mummification, and the famous Pyramids and Sphinxes. These developments were constantly reimagined and enhanced from one pyramid or sphinx to the next, from one period to another. To improve the quality of communication and record-keeping, between 2,000 and 5,000 characters formed the Egyptian hieroglyphic writing that is still a mystery to many today. There is evidence of surgical tools from those days that remain relevant in our world today, as well as the brilliant knowledge of astronomy and mathematics that respectively served as foundations for philosophical and architectural advancements in the modern world. All of these developments have been credited by many experts and scholars to the civilization of Ancient Egypt (Holmes, Ancient Egypt; Marshall Cavendish Corporation, 2011). While there is a lot that the world can boast over knowing about that ancient civilization, it is also believed that the magnificence and richness of that era have not been fully explored.

At the heart of all the richness, complexities, and glory of that era were the pharaohs of various dynasties who were charged with the advancement of their civilization. Some of them came down through historical records as hardly remarkable while the others, despite their imperfections, made their marks in undeniably significant ways. Throughout this book, we will explore the lives of these pharaohs, their extraordinary achievements and imperfections, and the lasting impacts of their reigns on the world today.

Chapter 1:

Understanding the General

Structure of Ancient Egypt

The history of Ancient Egypt is whole in and of itself. The existence of ancient Egyptians from the prehistoric periods to the entire course of their civilization nullifies all attempts to dismiss their stories as a kind of myth that is too grand a legacy for any people of African origin. The splendid civilization of ancient Egypt derives no validation from any other part of the world and has never sought such validation. Its failures and successes are entirely its own and require no comparison with any other civilization the world has known. If anything, the other parts of the world have been rather dutiful in following the leading steps of that ancient civilization.

Located in the northeastern part of Africa and shielded on all sides by the Nile River except to the north where the river empties into the Mediterranean Sea, the very beginning of Egypt and what we know today as Ancient Egypt (ca. 3100–332 B.C.E.) was a period generally known among historians, Egyptologists, and archeologists as prehistoric or predynastic. Reliable archeological evidence has already proven that the prehistoric period may have begun as far back as 8000 B.C.E. and that life during that time was unsurprisingly very simple. Many different hunter-gatherer tribes lived along and migrated toward the Nile River which served as a means of transportation from one part of Egypt to another, as well as a source of food and water for the communities near the area. At a previous time, hundreds of thousands of years before the Predynastic and Dynastic Periods when the climate was far from arid and the Sahara Desert was simply unimaginable, the hunter-gatherer tribes that lived and roamed the Egyptian territory basked in the colorful richness of the area.

In a little more than one thousand years before the Early Dynastic Period (ca. 3100–2686 B.C.E), the population that lived in the southern region of the Nile were known as inhabitants of Upper Egypt while those in the northern region were known as inhabitants of Lower Egypt. The environmental challenges of that period such as desiccation and desertification which caused more and more people to move toward the fertile banks, Delta, and Valley of the Nile played an important role in helping determine the habitable parts of Egypt that have lasted till this day. Considered a divine blessing, the annual late summer flooding of the Nile left behind rich black silt that covered and turned the fields and agricultural land into highly fruitful grounds for staple foods, such as barley and wheat, and vegetables, such as lettuce and cucumbers. To properly deal with the aftermath of the flood, a great display of communal cooperation was regularly employed. Canals and dykes were built and rebuilt to enhance the utilization of the water left by the Nile flooding, irrigation systems were cleared of waste, and the people generally had no problem with sharing among themselves. The expanding desert, also known as the *Red Land*, became a symbol of barrenness, death, and negativity, while the stretches of land where the Nile overflows, also known as the *Black Land*, became a symbol of abundance, good life, and positivity.

According to some scholars, the larger demographic of people in these areas were either native Africans or African migrants who had been forced to leave the harsh conditions of their previous settlements. Those migrants were still part of a budding African civilization that covered many stretches of land, including Egypt. In *The Destruction of Black Civilization*, renowned American Sociologist Chancellor Williams argued that "three-fourths of Egypt—or up to twenty-nine degrees north parallel" was part of the ancient Ethiopian empire, insisting that the "cradle" of the Egyptian civilization may actually be traced "further southward below the First Cataract [shallow stretches of rapids broken by hard stones at Aswan], centered around the cities of Napata and Meroe" from which "black civilization spread northward, reaching its most spectacular achievements in what became known as 'Egyptian Civilization'" (Williams, 1974, pp. 46-47).

Between ca. 6000 B.C.E. and ca. 4000 B.C.E., livestock and subsistence farming in Upper and Lower Egypt increased and fostered the build-up to the civilization that is the reason for a global fascination that has been described as "Egyptomania" in the present century and the last. Archeological discoveries have revealed that around that period, there were unique designs of arrowheads, stone palettes, and stone axes, as well as beautifully designed pots, jars, and cups that fostered the popularity of the Naqada culture and promoted inter-tribal and inter-regional trade. As the inhabitants of the north and south grew in numbers, so did the demand for water, fertile land, food, access to trade routes, understanding of their world through religious figures and deities, and several varieties of daily necessities increase. These daily necessities were lacking for many people of various racial groupings, from the Africans of the so-called "Upper Ethiopia," otherwise known as Egypt, to the Asians of the Far East and others.

According to Williams (1974), the daily needs of many different groups of foreigners had unavoidably driven them toward Egypt where nature was extraordinarily kind, making about 13,500 miles of land and open fields far more fertile than it would have been without the Nile overflow. In the view of Garland (2012, p. 27), "no other ancient people was so fortunate in terms of the environment" as the people of Ancient Egypt. For Williams (1974), the Nile overflow made the Egyptian territory "so rich in food production that it became world famous not only as the 'Bread Basket of the World' but also for its highly advanced civilization," (Williams, 1974, p. 52) leading to high levels of migration from other continents and the development of permanent mud and stone settlements, as well as the rise of clusters of political leadership in Upper and Lower Egypt. In Upper Egypt where kings were known as "King of Upper Egypt," Naqada and Hierakonpolis were the two centers where political power was concentrated, and in Lower Egypt where kings were known as "King of Lower Egypt," several native African and non-African racial groups, including Asians and Canaanites, held sway.

The Badarian Culture

The dominant artistic and cultural practices of the Predynastic Period four hundred years before 4000 B.C.E., or more generally between 5500 B.C.E and 3400 B.C.E., are believed to be indicative of the period when the Badarian culture flourished. Known to archeologists and many experts as a crucial Neolithic culture, the Badarian culture was set apart by its technological achievements as seen through the unique rippled pottery, rock-cut tombs, amulets, ceramics, flint tools, settlements, cemeteries, grave goods, stone tools, stone beads, and other artifacts found at predynastic sites and villages such as Hemamieh, Qau, Mostagedda, and Matmar—all of which are now washed, blown away, or buried under modern villages and farms (Vorster, 2016). Before the beginning of the Dynasties, the Badarian people of Upper Egypt demonstrated advancements in agriculture, impressive critical thinking and problem-solving skills, and the overall quality of their innovative minds through their artistic and sculptural works and fascinating artifacts of different kinds. In addition to farming, cattle herding, and fishing, their carving skills have also been found to be evident on cosmetic palettes and among grave goods such as figurines and animals carved into utensils and daily tools used for different activities (Vorster, 2016).

Discoveries from the grave goods have served as repositories of valuable information about the Badarian period to many Egyptologists and other experts in various fields. Because of those grave goods, which suggest the predynastic belief in the afterlife that would later become very popular during the Dynastic periods, analysts have been able to provide insights into the social, economic, religious, and political systems of that era. That the Badarians paid such great attention to the dead and their burial rituals meant that they saw the afterlife as not some kind of vacuum in which the dead are lost forever, but a world from which the dead can begin a new life and watch over those who are still alive on earth. For them, the dead were journeying to another world that was full of trials, wins, joys, and sadness, and they needed to be well prepared and have all the necessities for survival. Without the grave goods, the spirit of the dead would wander aimlessly in the afterlife, face extreme circumstances, make life uncomfortable for the living, and eventually be damned. One observation has explained how the philosophy of ancient Egyptians on the afterlife was more "a living science of death," than anything else, emphasizing that "in many ways, death was a series of tests, followed by something that was rather similar to actual life" (Van Basten, 2016).

Articles such as pottery, shell and stone necklaces, stone rings, ivory beads, alabaster, jasper, limestone, and so much more are part of the identified goods buried with the dead in hundreds of predynastic graves to accompany their spirits in the afterlife (Vorster, 2016). In particular, the highly skilled potters of the Badarian era—with pottery designs such as black-incised pottery, black-topped pottery, white cross-lined pottery, decorated pottery, and fancy forms pottery (Vorster, 2016)—have been credited with producing arguably the finest pottery of that era and many periods after. In addition, the Badarian people carried out commercial activities with people of other cultures living near and far from their settlements and immediate townships. Excavations have revealed how flint blades and copper tools from that era "sport handles with imagery that is decidedly Near Eastern in origin" and how "the existence of objects crafted of lapis lazuli (a material from Afghanistan) point to active trade between Egypt and western Asia" (Calvert, 2022).

The Naqada Cultures

The later part of the Badarian Period (ca. 4000–3000 B.C.E.) has been argued by some scholars to be interlinked with another period of cultural advancement known as the Naqada Culture which derived its name from Nubt, a town that famously translated as the "city of gold" in that ancient era. Remarkable progress was recorded during the predynastic Naqada periods, which can also be divided into three sub-periods: the Naqada I or Amaritian Period (ca. 4000-3500 B.C.E.), the Naqada II or Gerzean Period (ca. 3500–3200 B.C.E.), and the Naqada III Period (ca. 3200–3000 B.C.E.).

The fascinating thing about the Naqada periods was the cultural, political, technological, artistic, architectural, and other developments recorded in those periods. For example, the Naqada I period shared with the later part of the Badarian culture a general preference for shiny black-topped and polished red pottery, including a dazzling work of art like the polished red bowl that was shaped like a bird and another polished red bowl with human feet that had artistic, philosophical, and literary meanings. There were also many brilliant objects created from ivory and bones. Later periods of the Naqada culture would reveal brilliant advancements in pottery designs and the carvings of animals and humans on various types of pottery would become more and more popular. In addition, ceramic pots thrived in popularity throughout the whole Naqada era. These were coupled with sterling metalwork that produced tools for daily and extraordinary usage, such as the arrowhead and mace weapons used during unavoidable periods of warfare with hostile invaders.

The Naqada II and III periods revealed the determination of the predynastic people to make progress in building and craftwork. Sun-dried mud brick and clay houses were made in stronger and more beautiful shapes with various kinds of mud brick housing dedicated to local gods and goddesses, but because most of these structures were made with unfired clay, their durability was threatened by prolonged exposure to any severe flooding situation. Remarkable stone-cut reliefs were also made during this period, while discoveries have also revealed improvements in the technical details of burial sites and tombs. Progress was also made in economic activities, and some evidence of brilliant handicrafts, such as the shiny-eyed lapis lazuli figurine, suggest artistic progress, interactions, and trade with multiple foreign states from the Middle East to Asia.

Between ca. 4000–3200 B.C.E., a culture known as the Maadi Culture flourished in Lower Egypt with amazing progress made in the areas of animal domestication, agricultural systems, technological creations, settlements, development of customs, and commercial activities relating to copper that fostered economic relations with Upper Egypt and international trade with Mesopotamia and the Middle East. The Maadi culture also overlapped with Naqada II and III. During this period, burial customs developed a different approach for both adults and infants. Since the *Red Land* was considered the land of ghosts at this time, adults were more likely to be buried there than anywhere close to the inhabited townships. Infants, however, were more likely to be buried close to home in dedicated pits.

The Early Dynastic Period

The next phase of the history of ancient Egypt was shaped by the Early Dynastic Period, which marked the beginning of the Egyptian civilization under one gusty ruler generally known as King Narmer or Menes. According to Garland (2012, p. 25), a civilization generally means "centralized government, secure borders, settled conditions, artistic accomplishment, some technological knowhow, permanent structures, extensive contacts abroad, and an elaborate social hierarchy, all underpinned by a feeling of confidence in one's cultural identity," all of which was what Ancient Egypt was about and what undeniably made it one of the first civilizations in the world.

Through pictures, symbols, and the transcription of sounds, Egyptian hieroglyphics have provided us with reliable information on how the ancient civilization actually began. Between ca. 3200 B.C.E (or ca. 4000 B.C.E) and 3000 B.C.E., the people of the Nile Valley or Upper Egypt and the Nile Delta or Lower Egypt began to clash more often in a series of conflicts that gave Upper Egypt frequent wins, according to records on the Palermo Stone—an upright stone slab which enumerates the reigns of the kings of ancient Egypt from the Early Dynastic Period to the Old Kingdom. Before the reign of His Majesty King Narmer, discoveries show that one of the ancient leaders of Upper Egypt who was very close to uniting the Two Lands (Upper and Lower Egypt) was a warrior-king loosely known as Scorpion. At that time, Upper Egypt had become a successful kingdom and Lower Egypt was not far behind either, so the desire to expand their governed territories, develop a homogenous custom, and consolidate power continually led to conflicts between the two sides. For Williams (1974), the conflicts that led to the Unification of the Two Lands (some call it "Two Kingdoms")—and for some reason, this is a point that is hardly ever raised when talking about the Unification or the beginning of ancient Egyptian civilization—were more likely to have risen from the fact that one-fourth of Egypt had basically fallen under the control of the Asians and a small population of Arabs who were enslaving and shaming the Blacks in Lower Egypt. Williams (1974) explained this situation in this manner:

> In the Asian held areas in the north, the Blacks had hard choices to make. As elsewhere on the continent, they had the choice of remaining in their homeland and being reduced to the status of servants and slaves; or if they were well-to-do members of the professional classes, architects, engineers or skilled craftsmen, they could reject integration into Asian culture and migrate southwards. This the great majority did. (p. 64)

Carvings of flint blades, arrowheads, spiked maces or maceheads, and other representations of fighting tools, as well as scenes of wild animals devouring humans have been found at different tombs, cemeteries, and Early Dynastic Period sites in Upper Egypt, indicating the extended warfare that happened during that period between the region and possibly Lower Egypt. In one iconographic piece of archeological evidence famously known as the "Narmer Palette," the show of strength of the chief person of interest in the work of art, King Narmer or Menes himself, depicted him as a people's warrior—with his head covered with the crown of Upper Egypt and Lower Egypt—towering above the other people on the slab and particularly positioned with his raised mace to crush one of those believed to be either his enemy or one of the enemies of Upper Egypt. Also, there are those believed to be Narmer's enemies who are obviously without their heads in the visual images, indicating that he was a generally victorious warrior. Following Narmer's victory over the Nile Delta or Lower Egypt, more than 100,000 human captives and nearly two million animals were recorded to have been among his spoils.

While there are different opinions on the true meaning of the Narmer Palette, the clear message of warfare and victory has been upheld by many scholars, historians, and Egyptologists over the years. As a result, the Narmer Palette is considered the first evidence of an event of great importance generally referred to as the beginning of the Unification Period where King Narmer is regarded as the first "King of the Two Lands" or the first pharaoh of a united Egypt, and Memphis was the capital city. So great was the achievement of the Unification that it has been written that "during the king's coronation ceremony, which goes back to the founding of the capital at Memphis, the new king fired arrows towards the four cardinal points of the compass, and released birds to travel there to announce his rule" (Johnson, 2012).

With Narmer at the helm of affairs, a new era of administrative competence and institutional diligence was born. His achievements were numerous and he is widely credited with having set a great example of leadership and state building for his successors to follow. In this regard, Williams (1974) wrote:

> Menes [Narmer] brought about the kind of stability and innovations in administration that not only provided a solid foundation for a first dynasty, but also the economic and social conditions necessary for the more uniform expansion of religion, the arts, crafts and the mathematical sciences. (p. 67)

Narmer, though human, was seen by the people as a god, and the people followed his warnings, words, and decisions very strictly. While some people have interpreted the absolute authority of the Pharaohs as a sign of "totalitarian theocracy," the more popular viewpoint is that the Pharaohs were generally not far from the people. To place emphasis on this point, a widely respected scholar has written that "there was a good chance that ordinary Egyptians would set eyes on [the pharaoh] many times during the course of their lives" (Garland, 2012, p. 27). Under King Narmer's reign, there were several levels of administrative functions that signaled sharp progress from the comparatively lesser administrative duties required for just Upper Egypt. Some scholars have pointed out that this period was the first example and beginning of the notion of the nation-state as we know it today (Johnson, 2012).

It is also known that the bond between the family and the community became much stronger during the Early Dynastic period, and each relied on the other for physical, mental, spiritual, and other types of support. Unlike among pharaohs where marriage was sometimes complicated or done for the purpose of political advantage, as a symbol of peace, or other political reasons, the ordinary ancient Egyptians were generally more likely to marry for love than not. Young men and women were expected to marry early, and while the girls were considered ready for marriage from 12 years old upward, the boys could wait until they were 19 or after their circumcision from ca. 2500 B.C.E. onward. The children, if they did not die at birth or a young age, were expected to respect, obey, and assist their parents and elders in the community, as well as take care of their old parents and bury them according to custom when they die. This was usually the chief responsibility of the eldest son in the family. Graves of ordinary people many times were bare or without enough grave goods due to the lack of adequate resources, although the community sometimes supported different families in providing adequate grave goods for the dead. Rituals to the dead were a constant part of life in ancient Egyptian families and communities, as they believed the dead should be respected and made happy at all times. Although most ordinary people did not live longer than 35 years in ancient Egypt, there were strict dietary plans for the rich designed to make them live longer. However, most of them still didn't live above 50 years.

The rich families had household servants, and their children, unlike the children of families without adequate resources, were often not trained or required to work in the agricultural fields or perform any strenuous task. There were generally no social barriers between women and men as women were allowed to do almost anything the men could also do socially, including the right to own and inherit properties. However, when it came to the throne, the male hierarchy did not smile on women becoming kings or pharaohs. The relationship between men and women, especially with regard to norms on clothing and appearance, was rather interlinked. There are records of men using red ochre on their cheeks and kohl, a black cosmetic eyeliner, on their faces like women did. There are also records of men and women wearing the same wigs made from palm fibers, and jewelry was a major part of the culture of ancient Egyptians, whether man or woman, adult or child. Over time, the clothing for both men and women improved, starting arguably from the later part of the Early Dynastic Period with the men wearing *shendyt* while the women wore richly made, transparent *kalasiris*.

The literates who kept records of all official business and oversaw the transmission of official communication to the people, commonly known as scribes, were at the forefront of bridging the gap between the Pharaohs and the people. To reward them for their hard work on behalf of the state, the scribes and other officials in ancient Egypt relied on the agricultural produce of farmers, which was duly collected and parceled out not only to officials but also to priests and citizens who were limited by physical disabilities or duties of the state (Marshall Cavendish Corporation, 2011, p. 9). In this regard, the sense of communal living in ancient Egypt was very real.

Over the years, studies have shown that an important aspect of the life of ancient Egyptians during this early period was their huge sense of pride in their culture and identity. Of this, it has been said that the Egyptians "were among the first people—if not the first—to identify themselves as a people," meaning "they achieved cultural homogeneity based on a distinctive lifestyle and shared set of values rather than on any notion of blood relation" (Garland, 2012, p. 27). In another work by Johnson (2012), it is written that "[n]o culture in world history was so thoroughly penetrated by a quintessential style as the Egyptian." The richness of this cultural majesty was so profound that at a certain point the rate of migration to Egypt grew so high that an ancient Egyptian text lamented that "strangers from outside have come into Egypt… foreigners have become people everywhere" (Johnson, 2012).

At the center of this splendid Egyptian culture was a deep love for and reliance on theology. Many papyrus scrolls from ancient Egypt have survived to this day showing how much value the ancient Egyptians placed on understanding their world through the eyes of gods and goddesses, so much so that the Greek historian Herodotus wrote that "the Egyptians are more religious than any other people." Nearly 1,500 gods and goddesses have been identified to have been worshiped by ancient Egyptians, all created either from imagination or from those among the living who achieved extraordinary feats such as the kings who were perceived as divine beings. Some of these gods and goddesses can be traced as far back in history as the prehistoric period, and the fact of their survival throughout the ancient periods and today is proof of how these deities have been very central to the identity of the Egyptians. As it is sometimes the case for people in the 21st century to speak ill of the role and meaning of these deities in ancient Egypt, a cautious observation has been made by Wilkinson (2003) that:

> To the modern viewer this panoply of seemingly countless deities including animal, human, hybrid and composite forms with their kaleidoscopic symbols and attributes often appears strange and confusing at best and quite unintelligible at worst.

Yet closer examination reveals a world of interacting gods and goddesses whose myths and representations weave an amazing tapestry, often of unexpected intellectual and artistic sophistication. (p. 6)

The Pharaohs

For all that was quintessential Ancient Egypt, from the Unification Period until the very end of the civilization, a very large part of its grandness and grace came from the kings known as pharaohs. The breathtaking extent of their power and authority commanded respect both within the territories they ruled and far beyond. As symbols of divine authority, they spoke as mouthpieces of the gods, lived as the personification of the gods, and died to unite with Osiris, the god of the underworld. For ancient Egyptians, it was the divine duty of the pharaohs to be compassionate toward their people, to defend their rights internally and externally, and to uphold the Egyptian philosophy of propriety, social stability, and justice known as *Maat*. Enemies of the pharaohs were considered enemies of the entire state and the many gods watching over the pharaohs. The pharaohs ruled by lineages or dynasties, a turn-by-turn system to the throne that may or may not be inherited. It was the divine and royal duty of a pharaoh to produce an heir, which was where the Queen, called the "King's Wife" or "the Great Wife," of a pharaoh always came into the picture.

The pharaohs, starting with the Early Dynasty, demonstrated a remarkable capacity for critical and innovative thinking, which they used to set the civilization on a course of greatness for more than 3,000 years. To defend their territory, the pharaohs also waged wars against existing and potential enemies, quelling rebellions and foreign invasions and expanding the state's territories as often as possible. Since power during this period was concentrated at the center, outstanding systems of bureaucratic processes for a robust social organization and effective and transparent governance were set up by the pharaohs of the Early Dynastic period.

During their reigns as supreme rulers, the pharaohs commissioned and oversaw extensive projects, including massive buildings, sculptural works, temples, public infrastructures such as roads and transport networks, and tombs. In addition to their responsibilities in life, it was customary for the pharaohs to start planning for their own death by supervising the construction of their burial chambers right from the beginning of their reign (Van Basten, 2016). When the first pharaohs died, they were buried at the royal cemetery at Abydos—a city that was about 70 miles to the north of Naqada and has provided a large amount of valuable archeological evidence. Sometimes the pharaohs were buried with their retainers in what was known as a retainer ritual or ushabtis. They might also have been buried with their servants or, in rare cases, with their relations. The pharaohs were expected to continue their royal lives in the next world after they transition to the afterlife, which was why their grave goods frequently included any and all kinds of essential goods from drink and food to clothing, amulets, and art. However, this practice is believed to have not lasted long beyond the Early Dynasty.

Chapter 2:

An Explanation of Egyptian

Mythology and a Timeline

If there is one lesson we may proudly declare to have learned from history, it is perhaps the idea that even the most real things may sometimes need to be shielded by a body of myths. The reason for this can take the form of numerous interpretations, but history has shown us that myths can enhance people's understanding of themselves, increase their level of awareness of the supernatural world, beautify cultures and traditions, and serve as a source of inspiration for great achievements. Like most things in life, myths also require a modest level of responsibility from those they shield and colorize.

In ancient Egypt, mythology was oftentimes skillfully woven into the social fabric to create a rich cultural, social, political, and religious sense of awareness. For example, on the back of the Narmer Palette, there are carvings of various animals representing different mythological meanings. One account suggests that "the leopards with entwined serpentine necks might represent the joining of Upper and Lower Egypt" (Snape, 2021, p. 45). The wisdom of the people of ancient Egypt, in creating bodies of myths that would last for many generations and inspire a special relationship between the people and the objects of their creations, can be seen more in how they invented mythical figures. They aimed not to create flawless figures that people can hardly identify with. Rather, each of the mythical narratives was tied to the existence of something or someone, which originated from the people's real or imagined sense of their own existence.

The Gods and Society

There are scholars who believe that ancient Egyptian culture had its roots in the people's rich collection of myths, mostly religious. It is hard to argue against this point of view. The ancient Egyptians were masters at storytelling—a gift that was steeped in and nurtured from a complex and expansive world of mythical imagination. They told stories that inspired virtue, fear, courage, reverence, and dignity, but since it is the same people who own the culture, the myths, and the theology, it is probably more appropriate to say they created an unequaled world by interweaving culture, myths, and religious beliefs without any of the three having more significance than the others. For ancient Egyptians, there had to be a way for explaining everything from the sun and the moon to their existence, purpose on earth, and their duties and responsibilities to each other and the world in which they found themselves. To do this, they invented a story of creation which started with the god Ptah, who created the world from a shapeless surface of water known as the "Nu," alongside other gods, including Amun and Heh. An account of Egyptian mythology credits the god Amun with the power of validation of the words of Ptah. As a result, whatever name given to things by Ptah became the permanent names that not only helped identify them but, in most cases, also brought them to life. In another Egyptian myth, the father of Osiris, known as Geb, is believed to have angered his father Shu, who controlled all the forces in the air, when he married his sister, Nut, the sky goddess. In addition to Osiris, Geb and Nut also gave birth to other gods such as Seth, Nephthys, Isis, and Haroeris. These children were born despite Geb's separation from Nut, which was the result of a curse upon their union. Their father, out of jealousy, could not bear his pretty daughter marrying her brother and decided that Geb, the supreme ruler of the earth, would be permanently restricted to the earth while Nut would be permanently restricted to the sky. The couple found a loophole and with the help of the wisdom deity, Thoth, were able to meet and have children.

Another tragedy, also born of jealousy, was imminent in Geb and Nut's family: One of their children Seth, Osiris' brother who married his sister Nephthys, decided to kill his brother Osiris who had been recognized as the divine ruler of Egypt. To do this, Seth put Osiris into a large strongbox and drowned him in the Nile. As the myth goes, Seth was furious when Isis, his sister and wife of Osiris, found the dead body of Osiris after a difficult search. He took the corpse away from Isis, dismembered it, and scattered pieces of it across the land of Egypt, believing this would make it difficult for anyone to ever find Osiris as whole again. However, with the help of Seth's wife, Nephthys, Isis was able to use her divine power to stick the pieces of the dismembered Osiris together and resurrect him. This was how Osiris became known as the god of the land of the dead and the land of the living. As for Isis and Nephthys, they became goddesses of protection for the dead, just as they had protected the dismembered body of Osiris. Many ancient Egyptians requested that figurines of Isis and Nephthys be attached to their tombs, so they could have adequate protection on their way to the world of Osiris.

The story does not end there, though. Before Osiris passed away again—although, some say he never died again but simply took a walk back to the underworld—he managed to impregnate Isis, and she gave birth to a child they named Horus. Horus would become the ruler of Egypt but not without a last battle with his wicked uncle Seth. Horus had struggled on the throne as a young king, but he was constantly protected from his uncle's attacks by his father from the underworld. Seth believed he, not Horus, was the rightful heir to the throne and contested the throne until he was decisively defeated by Horus in adulthood. Horus would go on to rule Egypt for hundreds of years before he passed away and was reunited with his father Osiris in the underworld where all dead kings were believed to go when they passed away. Every king who ruled ancient Egypt after Horus became known as the successor to and the living evidence of Horus. Many of the pharaohs who later ruled Egypt across 30 dynasties had their given Horus name, starting with the name Narmer which meant "The Striking Catfish." Several millennia after the ancient Egyptian Osiris myth and myth of creation began, there are people who believe Osiris resurrects every year and still worship and celebrate the god in a festival known as the "Mysteries of Osiris" where they also pray to enjoy peace in the afterlife.

Early Kings

When King Narmer passed on to the world of Osiris, he was immediately succeeded by Aha or Hor-Aha, meaning "The Fighting Hawk," who was believed to be the son of Narmer and Queen Neithhotep. He ruled over the unified Upper and Lower Egypt and fought against the growing number of enemies of his state. His reign lasted for about six decades with several advances in trade and commerce, military, infrastructure, and architectural advancements credited to his name. He is also famous for his many visits to the temple of the goddess of wisdom and war, Neith, at Sais in the Nile Delta. During his reign, some of the largest boats were built, and according to different scholars (Clayton, 1994; Romer, 2013), his very large tomb at Abydos with storage rooms and underground chambers was evidence of a carefully achieved progress in the art of building tombs. One of the legends that has survived about King Aha says that he died after a scuffle with a hippopotamus, which was a popular animal to hunt in those days, especially for kings and people of the higher classes. He was buried with about 30 retainers who were believed to have accompanied him to the underworld.

In the Early Dynastic Period, there were a total of eight different kings after King Narmer—nine if we add the debated Queen Merneith, whose reign is surrounded by controversies among scholars. The king that immediately followed Hor-Aha was named Horus Djer or Djer, meaning "The Horus who Succors." He is likely the son of Hor-Aha and a woman named Khenthap who was probably one of the wives of Aha. He is believed to have reigned for 57 years during which he continued in the path of his predecessor, embarking on several military campaigns, building more infrastructure and making numerous visits to many temples. During his reign, there was what has been described as "an explosion" of skillfully made beautiful craftwork. Writing about this "explosion" period, which was not limited to Horus Djer's reign but largely included it, Romer (2013) has said:

> There were marvellous imitations of rush baskets and fig leaves cut from blocks of siltstone; hard-stone vases worked so finely that they obtained the luminosity of flowers; a range of

beauteous alabaster forms, jars and dishes such as were found in distant Byblos; and fine round offering tables and elegant tiny pots for oils and cosmetics. (p. 324)

When Horus Djer died, according to Clayton (1994), more than 300 retainers buried around his grand tomb accompanied him to the underworld. Later in the Middle Kingdom, the tomb would be rebuilt as a cenotaph for Osiris.

The one who followed in succession to the throne of Unified Egypt was known as Horus Djet, or "Horus Cobra," also known as Wadj or Uadji. Not much is known about this king except that his reign may have lasted, arguably, between 10 to 23 mostly peaceful years, although not without strategic attacks against Nubia, the arch-enemy of ancient Egypt located to the south of Egypt. One interesting bit is the fact that he married his sister Merneith, named after the goddess Neith, who would later become the regent who ruled over Egypt in place of her son, Den, after Djet's passing. The title of the regent is probably more appropriate for Queen Merneith since she was not known as a "Horus" king but as the "King's Mother." Of all the royals who ruled and lived during the First Dynasty, Queen Merneith was the only one who had two different royal tombs—one at the Saqqara necropolis of Memphis and the other at the Umm el-Qa'ab necropolis of Abydos—which suggests she may have been a really powerful and adored Queen. About 40 retainers were buried around her tomb at Abydos to accompany her to the underworld.

King Den, also known as "The Horus who Strikes," ascended to the throne at the appropriate age, and his reign lasted for at least 42 years. During his reign, several advances were made in writing, record keeping, taxation, and military expeditions. On an ivory label for him, he is standing over and attempting to crush an enemy from the east in a position similar to King Narmer's on his palette. His tomb has been described as "the largest and most finely built tomb in the Umm-el-Qaab necropolis of Abydos, consisting not only of the conventional mud bricks, but stone elements as well, such as a granite floor" (Livius, 2020). About 174 retainers were buried around his tomb to accompany him to the underworld.

Once Hor-Adjib or Anedjib, meaning "Safe is His Heart," ascended the throne, a host of controversies that would come to shape his reign began to swell. Although he was the son of Den and reigned for about 26 years, there may have been serious dynastic struggles during his reign. There was a battle of legitimacy between Upper and Lower Egypt, which some scholars have suggested also led to Anedjib marrying Queen Betrest of the Memphite line while he was from the Thinite line. In addition, this point of view is also supported by the fact of the shabby, small-sized tomb of Hor-Adjib and the extent of the defacement of the tomb and several objects of art initially designed with his name. Another viewpoint among scholars is one that links the serious division, particularly religious and cultural, that existed among the people of Egypt during Hor-Adjib's reign to the unusual emphasis he relentlessly placed on his title "Lord of the Two Lands," as if to prove that it was not in question. He similarly wore the double crown of Upper Egypt and Lower Egypt like his father Den. Also, the first basic idea of the Stepped Pyramid may have begun with the "stepped structure" at the tomb of king Adjib. He was buried with 64 retainers to accompany him to the underworld.

Hor-Adjib was succeeded by his son, Horus Semerkhet, meaning "Thoughtful Friend," who multiple sources suggest may have taken the throne by force, mainly because his name was not included in the Saqqara Tablet—a stone tablet with the list of kings who have ruled Egypt—although his name is included in the Palermo Stone. Records also show that the division and dynastic struggles under Hor-Adjib continued and worsened during Semerkhet's nine-year reign. However, there is reason to believe he also enhanced commerce and foreign trade during his reign, pushing the sale of ancient Egyptian bread molds and ceramics, among other things. In addition to these, it has been noted that since his death Semerkhet's tomb has been "saturated up to 'three feet' deep with aromatic oil" that was possibly of Syrian-Palestinian origin (Shaw, 2003). The account would go further to say (Shaw, 2003):

> The presence of such huge quantities of oil in Semerkhet's tomb (perhaps in the course of his funeral ceremony) certainly suggests its very large-sale foreign trade controlled by the crown and indicates the importance of such luxury goods for royal burials.

Horus Qa'a (meaning "His Arm is Raised") was the last of the kings of the 175 years of the First Dynasty, and the reason for this is usually traced to the growing division in Egypt, which started during the reign of Hor-Adjib. Qa'a was probably the son of Semerkhet, and his reign lasted between 23 to 25 years. Although his name was not omitted from the Saqqara Tablet, his tomb at Abydos is believed to have gone through many phases of alteration. About 26 retainers were buried around his tomb, but the practice of retainer ritual likely ended with his reign.

From the Third Dynasty to the Sixth

The period between the Third Dynasty to the Sixth (ca. 2686–2181 B.C.E.), also known as the Old Kingdom (not including the Seventh & Eighth Dynasties) and the Age of Pyramids, was a period of tremendous progress in the history of ancient Egypt. It was the period when the struggles of legitimacy that dogged the previous years had largely reduced and the focus had begun to shift to designing broader and much more effective administrative systems that would enhance the economic, cultural, and religious outlooks of the ancient people toward building a peaceful and prosperous civilization. It was during the four dynasties of the Old Kingdom that some of the monuments and architectural landmarks that remain thrilling to those who are alive today were built. These range from the Stepped Pyramid, the Sphinx, and Great Pyramid to the historic sites in Dashur, Saqqara, and Giza, now known as the tomb sites of many great kings in ancient Egypt. As mightily and powerfully as the dynasties had pushed up the state of ancient Egyptian civilization to tremendous heights from the Fourth to the Fifth Dynasty, there would come a period of decline in the strength of the civilization in the Sixth Dynasty, causing a breakup of the unified state and the rise of local chiefs and nobles.

For about 18 or 19 years, the first king of the Third Dynasty, known as Nebkha or Horus Sanakhte, meaning "Victorious Protector," ruled ancient Egypt. Generally, what is known or not known about him is recorded with caution as there is no complete certainty about his existence, the nature of his ascension to power (there are some arguments that he forced his way to the throne), or his exact family line. Some scholars and Egyptologists have suggested that he was the older brother of King Djoser, his successor, but there are others who believe his reign was between King Djoser and the last king of the Third Dynasty, King Huni. There are also those who believe that Nebkha and Sanakhte are two different kings and do not include Nebkha's name at all in their works, but a mastaba from Beit Khallaf has been identified without any certainty to be his tomb.

The king that followed Nebkha, according to the records, was king Djoser (also known as Horus Netjerikhet, meaning "Divine of Body") who was possibly the son of Nimathaap ("mother of the king") and Khasekhemwy and the last king of the Second Dynasty. One of the unforgettable things about Djoser's nineteen-year reign was the fact that it brought a lot of architectural projects to life, including the Stepped Pyramid and the Mortuary Complex of Djoser. The Djoser complex is famous for a lot of things, the least of which is its very massive structure. It contains 14 fake doors of which only one grants access to the complex. In the Sinai Peninsula, Djoser made a lot of progress economically, including using copper and other minerals from the peninsula for economic growth. Although he was not keen on military campaigns, he used the peninsula as a buffer zone between ancient Egypt and West Asians (the "shoulder-knot people") and Arabs, securing it for trade and commerce. The result of his wisdom to focus on economic success can be seen in the attainment of his extremely difficult goals of building his pyramid and complex within 19 years. The responsibilities that his government must have taken in order to cater to the size of manpower his architectural projects alone required could not have been done with a weak base of economic resources. There is no doubt that the fact that he focused less on warfare and promoted the internal growth of the state opened up the doors to new ideas and advances in education, writing, economy, and politics, including bringing competent people from humble backgrounds into government positions. In many ways, he was a visionary.

The story of Djoser would be incomplete without mentioning Imhotep, his architect, high priest, and special adviser. With Imhotep by his side, Djoser was able to achieve unprecedented achievements that are still relevant more than 4,000 years later. For example, there was a serious famine that lasted for about seven years in ancient Egypt during Djoser's reign, and the people suffered untold hardship due to the famine. Imhotep felt the famine was one of the consequences of falling into disfavor with the god of the Nile and fertility, Khnum. He would offer his humble advice to King Djoser to visit Elephantine in Upper Egypt and build a temple for Khnum to appease the god. It was recorded that the famine stopped after king Djoser built the temple, and the people's admiration of the king increased tremendously. The reputation of Imhotep, a man from very humble beginnings, would also take a turn for the better after the temple was built. What really turned Imhotep into a hero, though, was the fact that he was the architect who built a 200-foot-tall monument, the Stepped Pyramid at Saqqara, which was the tallest in the world at that time. The Stepped Pyramid was a genius work for its time. It was a construction that reproduced the mastaba in a series of layers using more than 500,000 tons of limestone, among other important elements, making it the first of its kind worldwide. It was breathtaking in size and was considered a work of divine inspiration by the ancient Egyptians, which was why dedication rituals to the gods became a big part of the pyramid-building process. Long after his death, more than 2,000 years after, there were still people in Egypt who worshiped Imhotep as an Egyptian god.

Before 1951, several accounts from multiple Egyptologists attest that virtually nothing was known about Horus Sekhemkhet, meaning "Powerful of Body," the successor to King Djoser. Of what would later be known about him, there is little to add apart from his unfinished pyramid and the suggestion that his reign as king may have been very short, some say around six years, even though his pyramid was likely to have surpassed Djoser's had it been finished. Mostly, more is known about Sekhemkhet's tomb than his activities while alive. Also, the records do not say much about the life of king Khaba and king Huni, who were respectively the ones who followed king Sekhemkhet in ascending the throne. Horus Khaba also had an unfinished pyramid in Zaqiyet al-Aryan, not far at all from Saqqara. King Huni built some small pyramids, but the pyramid that was close to his heart, the one at Maidum, was not finished before he died.

The story gets a lot more interesting at the beginning of the Fourth Dynasty. It is the dynasty that gave birth to the Red Pyramid and several other structures with enormous sizes and incredible visions from Dashur to Maidum. The dynasty started with king Snefru or

Sneferu, meaning "He of Beauty." He was also known as Horus Neb-Maat, meaning "Lord of the Cosmological Order," and he was the son of King Huni of the previous dynasty. Snefru is mostly remembered for his successful attempts to build pyramids that were more advanced than those of his predecessors, but he was also very close to his people and was widely adored for his kind heart. In places like Sinai and parts of the Middle East where he sometimes traveled, he was seen as a god and worshiped as one. A story narrates how he ordered one of his advisers who was also a magician to retrieve a lost trinket for a maiden of his court. The trinket was found at the bottom of a lake and restored to the court maiden who became happy and went on with her day, pleasing the king.

Snefru also embarked on some military campaigns against the Libyans and Nubians and won on multiple occasions, creating a strong state with a vibrant economy for his son to inherit. Snefru would go on to build a series of very small Stepped Pyramids and call forth his innovative mind to create before unseen pyramid designs. The more popular pyramids attributed to Snefru such as the Red Pyramid and the smooth Bent Pyramid at Dahshur became inspirational models for subsequent kings and their visions of future pyramids. The Red Pyramid is the second largest pyramid by area at Giza, following the Great Pyramid built by Snefru's son, Khufu. It was the first pyramid to take the triangular shape of the later pyramids, and the "red" is said to glow under the sun. Snefru married his sister, Hetepheres, mainly to give legitimacy to his reign since his mother, Meresankh, was not from a royal background. He would leave behind a very powerful state to his son, Khufu, after a reign that lasted for about 24 years.

Khufu is one of the most popular pharaohs we know from ancient Egypt. He was the son of King Snefru and Queen Hetepheres and the successor to King Snefru. He must have grown up very ambitious. From the moment he took the throne, Khufu, also known as Cheops, set his eyes on building monuments greater than those of his father and the other rulers before him. He started off by finding a different location for his monuments and complex away from the Saqqara necropolis and the site of his father's pyramid, Dashur. He is sometimes said to have been a cruel king who disrespected the gods and had no interest in their veneration. Although he was also accused of building his pyramid and other structures with slaves, there are multiple sources attesting to the opposite, clarifying that he duly rewarded the workers and also used the services of very skillful artisans who were also well rewarded. His Horus name, Medjedu, meaning "the one who hits," is appropriate considering his warlike foreign policy.

Like his father, Cheops focused on military expeditions to expand his territory and also established a strong presence in the Sinai Peninsula and other territories that were strategic to his goals. In terms of trade and commerce, he was a visionary economist who not only created policies for internal economic growth but also entered into trade deals with foreign states, including Nubia where he sometimes engaged in military battles. As proof of his greatness, his Great Pyramid at Giza, one of the Seven Wonders of the World, covered about 13 acres of land, and it was about 481 ft tall, making it the tallest structure in the world at that time, by completion with remarkable precision to the cardinal points. His reign is disputed to have lasted between 23 to 33 years, but he is said to have had a change of heart with regard to his respect for the gods and wrote Sacred Books that would become one of the main pieces of literature to come out of ancient Egypt. He had at least two queens, Queen Henutsen and Queen Meritites, and many sons and some daughters. Also, it would seem some of his retainers were buried around his corpse, although the practice had become quite rare at that point in ancient Egypt. His mother was buried not far from his tomb since her original burial place was half-robbed by tomb robbers. Trinkets and golden artifacts were found in what was left of the large box in her sarcophagus. It was later discovered in the early twentieth century that, despite his profound commitment to building the Great Pyramid, Khufu also built a wooden ship.

When Khufu passed on, there was a power struggle among his sons. According to some accounts, his eldest son, Kauab, had a very short reign since he was probably assassinated. Another son of Khufu was said to have ascended the throne after Kauab, but he, too, only held the throne for a brief period before Djedefre, also known as Kheper (meaning "Horus Has Become"), took the throne and ruled for about eight to eleven years. He was the second to adopt the title "son of Re" (a sign of great reverence for the sun god) between the First Dynasty and the Fourth Dynasty and to specifically use the title in the Fourth Dynasty. The theory that Djedefre succeeded Khufu, particularly because Kauab died while he was still a crown prince, is probably more popular than the other theories. His name, Djedef-re, means "Enduring like Re." There are scarcely any records on his or his brothers' reign, but it is known that he built a pyramid at Abu Rawash. Next came Khafre (Chephren), who was more like his father, Khufu, in being ambitious. He was the son of Queen Henutsen, and his Horus name, Weser-ib, means "Horus, who is strong of heart." Records have shown that his reign was peaceful, fairly long, lasting about 26 years, and fruitful. The economy, technology, and the arts flourished during his reign. He was also religious and worshiped Re like his predecessor. This can be deduced from his name which means "Appearing like Re." However, he is more popular today for building the Giza Plateau Great Sphinx and the Second Pyramid.

Following Khafre, Mankaure ascended to the throne, having watched Bakare, his uncle, perish on the throne after a very short reign in power. Menkaure (Mycerinus), meaning "Eternal like the Souls of Re," built the Third Pyramid at Giza and reigned for about 28 years. He was married to Queen Khamerernebty II and two other unknown Queens. Little is known about Shepseskaf (meaning "His Soul is Noble") who reigned for four years after Menkaure. His mother is probably one of the unknown Queens who married Menkaure, but there are remarkable works of art, very full of life, which survived him. Some were found at his tomb at Saqqara named Mastaba el-Faroun.

The rest of the Fourth Dynasty is buried in mystery which is still unknown, but the dynasty ran its course shortly after Menkaure. Apparently, there had been a prophecy that gave birth to a pact between the High Priest of Re and King Khufu. The prophecy said that after Khufu's reign, his son and grandson would rule and then yield the throne to three children of Reweddjedet, the wife of the High Priest of Re, and they will be of Heliopolitan origin like their mother. The first three kings of the Fifth Dynasty—Userkaf (ca. 2498–2491 B.C.E.), Sahure (ca. 2491–2477 B.C.E.), and Neferirkare (ca. 2477–2467 B.C.E.)—were believed to have fulfilled this pact. However, there is a theory that since Userkaf married Menkaure's daughter and Shepseskaf's half-sister, Khentkawes, the two dynasties were interconnected.

During the Fifth Dynasty, there was a shift away from building pyramids toward building temples and focusing on religious practices, particularly the worship of the sun god Re, which led to an explosion of the cult of Re. The kings of the Fifth Dynasty are commonly called the "Sun Kings." Although the period may not have been as remarkable as the Fourth Dynasty, it was still very important to the progress of ancient Egyptian civilization ranging from the solar temples at Abu Gorab and Abusir built for the sun god and the small pyramids and complexes built by the successors of Userkaf to the pyramid texts found at Saqqara in the pyramid of Unas, the last king of the Fifth Dynasty. The pyramid texts of the Fifth Dynasty were the first of their kind and quickly became a trend for successive kings. The texts included hundreds of spells believed to be part of the rituals performed to accompany the dead to the afterlife. Subsequently, the texts would play a crucial role in the development of the "Book of Emerging Forth Into the Light," to be later known as the "Book of the Dead" papyrus. When Unas died, he had no son to inherit the throne, which accelerated the chaos that brought about the end of the Fifth Dynasty and a long period of political unrest. It would take the arrival of King Teti of the Sixth Dynasty to restore order and peace in the state.

The Sixth Dynasty (ca. 2345–2181 B.C.E.) brought back peace, stability, and a powerful central government, which came with the reign of Teti or Sehetep-tawy (meaning "He who pacifies the Two Lands"), the first king of the dynasty. To enhance peace and continue enjoying the support of the nobility, Teti married his daughter Sesheshet to his vizier Mereruka who built a large tomb with about 32 rooms for himself at Saqqara. Teti himself married Ipwet, the daughter of Unas, for political legitimacy. He recorded successes in trade and commerce and possibly fought zero wars, instead adopting diplomacy as his strategy for maintaining peace. His reign lasted for about 11 or 12 years before he was allegedly murdered by his bodyguards, and Userkare, of whom nearly nothing is known, took the throne for a short time. Subsequently, King Teti's son, Pepi I would ascend the throne after Userkare's demise and rule for a long time, about 50 years.

Pepi I, also known as Merytawy ("He who loves the Two Lands"), had a different approach to foreign policy and launched attacks and established garrisons in places like Nubia, Sinai, and parts of the Middle East. He was also known for building temples in Abydos and other places, as well as building a large pyramid in Saqqara and a copper statue. Unlike the Fifth Dynasty in which the sun god was worshiped,

Pepi I was known for worshiping and building temples for Hathor, the goddess of fertility, love, and pleasure. During the reign of Pepi I, there was a harem conspiracy to kill him involving Queen Weret-Imtes, his first wife. King Pepi I appointed his trusted advisor, Weni, to judge the case as he saw fit. The Queen was killed after she was found guilty. Weni was likely a wise man who, like Imhotep, diligently worked his way up from humble beginnings to the highest positions in court before becoming a commander of the army.

After the death of King Pepi I, his oldest son Merenre ascended to the throne, but he did not sit on it for long, lasting only about seven years. Then came Pepi II, the son of Queen Ankhnesmerire II who became the youngest and the last strong king of the Sixth Dynasty. He ruled for more than 90 years, having ascended the throne at the age of 6, while his mother served as the regent until he was old enough. During the second half of his long reign, power became weaker at the center, and the strength of the economy declined despite maintaining the garrisons and having different viziers for Upper Egypt and Lower Egypt to help him consolidate power. His mortuary complex was built at Saqqara, and it is believed to be indicative of the problems of the last days of his reign because it was poorly made. What followed Pepi II's reign was a broken state with numerous clusters rising as centers of power across Upper Egypt and Lower Egypt. The subsequent period of crisis, which lasted from the Seventh Dynasty to the Eleventh Dynasty, is what is known as the First Intermediate Period. The crisis period lasted for a little more than 120 difficult years.

The Second Intermediate Period

Apart from the deep political crisis of the time, the ancient Egyptians emerged from the Old Kingdom as masters of many things. Their spirit of enterprise and ingenuity had created myths and stories far beyond the entire boundaries of the Egyptian state. In addition to the extraordinary problem-solving skills they demonstrated to meet the very harsh demands of their time, they were able to create a supreme image for themselves, architecturally in particular with regard to the pyramids. One observation has noted that "the pyramid was, to a large degree, the supreme demonstration of the power of the Egyptian state in the early Old Kingdom" (Snape, 2021). It is difficult to argue with that conclusion because the pyramids of the Old Kingdom were more than just structures of imposing sizes that were very unusual for their time. They had become symbols of complex communication between the living and the dead, symbols of greatness in life and in the afterlife.

On the walls of these pyramids, the diversity of ancient Egyptian literature was on full display, creating an awe-inspiring and all-consuming effect on the living. The ancient Egyptians saw the pyramid texts, selected and inscribed on pyramid walls from a large body of Egyptian literature, as a way of protecting the spirits and souls of the Pharaohs. The pyramid texts were magical inscriptions that transported the impacts of powerful spells from life to the afterlife. The texts were diligently inscribed by the hundreds, and they covered pyramid corridors, chambers, sarcophagi, and the resting places of the kings to send the kings to a world shining under the bright light of the sun or the remarkable beauty of the stars. To explain the powerful uniqueness of the spells in the pyramid texts, it has been written by Snape (2021) that:

> A particularly important set of spells summoned the king to rise from his sarcophagus and join the gods. His journey was a version of the journey of the sun god, Ra, who travels through the darkness of the Duat (underworld) to emerge reborn into the light of day. (p. 71)

After the Old Kingdom ran its course, the pyramid texts became more popular and royals and powerful families known as courtiers also began using inscription of spells, known as Coffin Texts, during their burial rituals. Eventually, the texts would become more and more popular among the wider population, all of whom wanted a smooth journey to the afterlife and an even smoother experience in that afterlife. Surviving information on how the Egyptians lived during that period of division reveals how middle-class people who were following in the footsteps of the kings and nobles also had those sacred texts inscribed on their "box coffins," which were discovered in large cemeteries in large numbers. In addition to the texts, the ancient Egyptians had highly gifted artists and painters who made beautiful and long-lasting paintings on the tombs, mastabas, and pyramids of royals and courtiers. The creativity started with the random properties of nature at their disposal such as natural pigments, mineral elements, and so much more. Those paintings displayed the richness of the life of the kings and other royals, and they ranged in subject from animals to dancers and singers and even the royals themselves. The grandness of the pyramids and the richness of the texts and paintings were signs of the weaknesses and strengths of the king who ruled when they were made. Egyptologists believe that the bigger pyramids and richer texts and paintings were made during the reigns of strong kings while the opposites were made during the reigns of the weak kings. Some scholars rely on these signs to understand the weaknesses that led to the collapse of the Old Kingdom and the endurance of 800 years of centralized power.

The period that followed the collapse of the Old Kingdom, known as the First Intermediate Period, was a period of great chaos and instability. The regional leaders who took over the helm in their respective regions, known as nomes, were constantly at war with one another and jostled for control both within and beyond their nomes. The crisis of the First Intermediate Period was a crisis that had huge consequences. It affected the economic, social, and political structures of ancient Egypt, and it was a period of shortage and suffering, especially for ordinary people. Famine, economic hardship, grave robberies, tribal and regional warfare, civil wars, opportunistic power blocs, and constant political conspiracies were all features of that unstable period. This period of great hardship, suffering, disunity, and chaos gradually continued but wavered in intensity, particularly toward the end of the First Intermediate Period and at the early stage of the Middle Kingdom (the Twelfth Dynasty). During this time a relatively strong central power was established at Thebes in Upper Egypt, followed by the unification of the Two Lands again, until the arrival of the Second Intermediate Period, which followed the Middle Kingdom.

During the Twelfth Dynasty, ancient Egypt recorded some really remarkable progress in social and cultural life, and the arts also enjoyed impressive growth. Some of these advances were made during the reigns of Mentuhotep II and Senwosret III, who fought battles to expand their territory, established more Egyptian control over different parts of Nubia, and built clusters of military strongholds while gathering massive resources out of those conquered territories, which included Lower Nubia. Mentuhotep II became a powerful Theban king in his time and dedicated his reign to rebuilding the previously divided Egyptian state. He rebuilt different structures at the necropolis in Abydos which had been destroyed during the intense wars with Nubia, Sinai, Libya, and other rivals. He also built a funerary complex and statues which survived him and became lasting proof of his great reign of about half a century. By the time he died, the practice of having co-regents while the reigning king was still in power had become a central part of the ruling system, which helped to stabilize the previously divided state. Archeological evidence also suggests that some soldiers who died fighting in his wars and battles had the privilege of being buried close to the king. Like Mentuhotep II, Senwosret III focused on consolidating power at the center by limiting the powers of the local leaders and nomarchs. He also led many battles against multiple enemies ranging from Nubia where there was an alleged uprising against the ancient Egyptian empire at the time to Palestine and Syria. In the place of the local leaders and nomarchs, he empowered merchants and farmers, and the social status of many of these people improved under his reign. He was succeeded by Amenemhet III whose interest in battles was not as great as his interest in building large structures such as temples, statues, the Black Pyramid (which he sadly did not complete), irrigation structures, and what was probably the largest pyramid of the Middle Kingdom. However, toward the end of his reign, things began to fall apart, and the entire Middle Kingdom would follow not long after. The daughter of Amenemhet, Queen Sobekneferu, is recorded as the last pharaoh of the Middle Kingdom. Her reign began after the death of her husband, Amenemhet IV, and the fact of her reign as the first Queen who had the support of all the powers at the time can be found in the records. She was devoted to Sobek, the Egyptian god of crocodiles and the Nile creation, and raised a cult in his name. She is believed to have reigned for approximately four years.

The disintegration of the Middle Kingdom into chaos opened the door to the larger confusion and power struggles of the Second Intermediate Period. According to the records, the Thirteenth Dynasty, which lasted between 116 to 123 years and had between 50 to 65 kings, was a period of numerous weak kings. The majority of them were unrelated, and their areas of control were mostly regional. Some of them were complete foreigners and others were locals who came from families of different social statuses, although those from rich or high-class families often dominated the others during this period. A huge part of this confusion and chaos is believed to have happened because of the so-called Hyksos, meaning "rulers of foreign lands," but multiple records have confirmed that the majority of the Hyksos initially settled in Egypt as migrants, while the others were forced there as slaves from conquered territories. As time went on, the Hyksos began to gain more ground either by marrying the locals or through political negotiations. They would eventually become so powerful that they were able to seize power for themselves as Egypt's unity broke down toward the end of the Middle Kingdom. There were hardly any remarkable events in the Second Intermediate Period. It was largely shaped by the generally short reigns of coexisting dynasties and the domination of the Hyksos, which started in Avaris, their capital, in the Nile Delta. The Hyksos were in a continuous power struggle with the Thebans and provincial rulers in different parts of ancient Egypt and made themselves powerful while the state was generally weak. The Hyksos King Ipep, named after the Egyptian god Apepi who was mostly regarded as an arch enemy of Re, started a war with Tao II, the king in Thebes, which signaled the beginning of the end of a mostly Hyksos domination since the Thirteenth Dynasty. By the end of the Seventeenth Dynasty, the Hyksos kings and their armies had been pushed farther from the Nile Delta, and ancient Egypt was nearing the beginning of a new era that we now know as the New Kingdom.

The New Kingdom

In the Eighteenth Dynasty, the Early New Kingdom began with King Ahmose, who ascended to the throne at the age of 10 as the brother of the last king of the Seventeenth Dynasty, Kamose. The New Kingdom was a period of liberation, renaissance, and prosperity for ancient Egyptians. It was the period when warrior kings and warrior queens stood their ground to fight for their land, their people, and their rights. It was a period of great social, political, religious, and cultural advancements. Ahmose, the first king of this period, is famous for three things. One, he united Upper and Lower Egypt again and began an era that took the Egyptian civilization to greater heights. Two, he finished what his brother Kamose and the previous kings had started: pushing out the Hyksos completely. Three, he built the last known

Royal pyramid in Abydos, but he did not do this alone. He had the support of his family, especially the women, among whom was his mother who led the Theban army against the Hyksos. He built a tomb and funerary complex in honor of her courage and contribution to their liberation from the Hyksos. Apart from these achievements, he delegated power and responsibilities a lot to provincial representatives while he embarked on different military campaigns in Nubia and the Middle East. He was also a very religious king known to have built multiple temples for different Egyptian gods. He died at the age of 35, which was not unusual as life expectancy was ridiculously low in those days.

Following his reign, the power of Egypt in the New Kingdom would only grow stronger. The roles of women in the rise of Egypt in this period were very prominent. Like men, they went to war, rose to the throne, became powerful and feared politically, and some were even made goddesses after their death. Amenhotep I ascended to the throne when his father Ahmose died. He was known for his strong will and commitment to concentrating political power at the center to avoid the troubles that led to the First Intermediate Period. He secured Egypt and built many temples and structures. When he died, Theban priests made him a god. After him, there was Thutmose I, Thutmose II, Thutmose III, Hatshepsut, Amenhotep II, Thutmose IV, Amenhotep III, Amenhotep IV, Smenkhkare, Tutankhamen, Ay, and Horemheb. After this came the Nineteenth Dynasty and then the Twentieth Dynasty of many Ramesses in the late New Kingdom, which led ancient Egypt right into another period of extensive chaos known as the Third Intermediate Period.

The Third Intermediate Period had many kings and pharaohs who ruled different parts of Egypt at the same time. From the Tanis pharaohs and Theban priests to the reigns of the Kushites and the Libyans, to the numerous wars and battles for political and economic power. In the Late Period that followed and lasted from the Twenty-Sixth Dynasty to the Thirty-First Dynasty, there were numerous changes in Egypt, and the civilization was shaped by the rise and fall of kings and dynasties and the reigns of weak and strong kings, which eventually led to the reign of the last Egyptian king in the Thirtieth Dynasty. Too many wars and battles had devastated Egypt and reduced its power politically and economically. Persians and Greeks constantly attacked and invaded Egypt, and with time the Persians conquered and ruled Egypt for a few decades.

By the end of the Thirty-First Dynasty, which is also known as the Second Persian Period, the Egyptian civilization had been significantly weakened, and the last Persian King Darius III would be defeated by Alexander the Great from Macedonia. Alexander is generally known as a visionary who not only built cities and massive structures in Egypt but also respected the culture and religion of the Egyptian people, although he mostly ruled Egypt by proxy through satrapies and the Ptolemies. Two other kings from Macedonia ruled Egypt after the death of Alexander before the reigns of the Ptolemies between 305 B.C.E. to 30 B.C.E. The Ptolemaic Dynasty was ruled in succession by descendants of the lineage, including Cleopatra VII, although there were many political conflicts in between. The Romans would completely take over the control of Egypt in 30 C.E., making it part of the famous Roman Empire until its fall around 395 C.E.

Chapter 3:

A Brief Timeline of the Most

Powerful and Feared Pharaohs and

Rulers of Ancient Egypt

Throughout the course of ancient Egypt, the great civilization was shaped and directed by the courage and vision of many strong rulers. Their leadership, strength, and charisma inspired the people in many different ways that resulted in innovative and breathtaking changes to society, culture, and politics. Among the copious number of rulers and pharaohs of ancient Egypt from the Predynastic Period to the Late Period and even the Greco-Roman Period, there were rulers and pharaohs of extraordinary character, strength, courage, and vision who impacted the history of ancient Egypt in unforgettable ways. They were rulers who inspired devotion and admiration and caused many to fear them for their greatness. In this chapter, we will briefly look at their lives and how they influenced the civilization of ancient Egypt.

Ramesses II

Ramesses II, also known as Ramesses the Great, was a man of great fame and many achievements. To this day, his fame and greatness have continued to echo throughout Egypt and different parts of the world. After being a co-regent to his father Seti I, he reigned between 1279 B.C.E. and 1213 B.C.E. during the Nineteenth Dynasty in the New Kingdom. He was famous for his ostentation, military exploits, spirit of adventure, monuments, and other architectural marvels, as well as his love for women. For around 67 long years of reign, Ramesses II made a mark on ancient Egypt as one of the most unforgettable pharaohs to ever rule the Unified Two Lands. He built structures, colossuses, temples, cities, and monuments that bore his name in different styles of engravings that have lasted for millennia; although, the projects and his ostentatious lifestyle put a great burden on the state's finances. At Abu Simbel, which is close to the border of Egypt and Sudan today, the temples built by Ramesses II—the Temple of Ramesses II and the Temple of Queen Nefertari—can be found with impressive statues that are full of life and multidimensional effects. The extraordinary talents of the ancient Egyptians can be seen through these structures, especially considering the fact that the temples had once been cut into more than 1,000 pieces and relocated from their original site to their current site. The relocation was done to protect the structures from being buried under the Aswan High Dam, which was built in Aswan in Upper Egypt to serve the multipurpose of being a source of electricity and keeping the Nile Flooding in check, while also serving as a most advantageous irrigation system. Ramesses II is also credited with contributing the Great Hypostyle Hall, the temple of Karnak, and the sacred temple of the god of creation, Amun, as well as another contribution to the complex in ancient Thebes hosting the Luxor Temple. He also completed his father's temple at Abydos and built himself a funerary complex that was not far from it.

All the monuments built by Ramesses the Great, including some of the structures built before his reign, have engravings of his name in large and deep styles. He was a man with a big ego and he thrived shamelessly on it. He was so in love with structures and monuments that he even claimed some structures built by his father and grandfather as his own and engraved his name in large forms on them. One of the reasons he has remained very famous to this day is because he had a total number of 200 wives in his harem, among whom was his most beloved and the first of the Great Royal Wives of the King, Queen Nefertari, who was also a very famous Queen in her own right. He is believed to have fathered between 96 and 100 sons, as well as 60 daughters. His first and dearly loved wife, Nefertari, was a descendant of the Hittites against whom Ramesses II waged several wars before the two sides finally signed a peace deal 21 years after he became the ruler of Egypt. He had multiple grandchildren, although 12 of his sons died while he was alive. Ramesses was deified and worshiped as a god. He died at the age of 90.

Amenhotep III

The ninth pharaoh of the Eighteenth Dynasty and the New Kingdom was Amenhotep III. He ascended to the throne at the age of 12 around 1388 B.C.E. and served the people of ancient Egypt for 38 years of peace and great cultural, artistic, and economic achievements and prosperity. The son of Thutmose IV and a lesser wife named Mutemwiya, Amenhotep III followed in his father's footsteps to build an empire that thrived economically and artistically. His father had focused more on religious and cultural advancements and less on the military and warfare. In fact, his father reduced his military size to cut down on government spending for the army and focused on building a vibrant civil service that would make life smoother and more prosperous for the people. When Amenhotep III became pharaoh, he also reduced the size of his military and invested heavily in the arts and the development of effective communication systems in an ever-growing government. He was a king who favored a diplomatic and non-aggressive foreign policy, and his harem of lesser wives who were daughters of the kings of other states reflected this policy. His first wife, Queen Tiye, who was about six years old when Amenhotep married her, was dearly loved by the pharaoh, and together they brought the next king, Akhenaton, to life. During his reign, Amenhotep III focused heavily on building his economy by mining gold in Nubia and pushing whatever limits may have existed on foreign trade before his reign, and this particularly favored him since he was known as a king who loved peace.

This does not mean Amenhotep III was in any way weak or less powerful. His power was great, and his strength and vision lifted ancient Egypt to many great heights. The economic achievements he recorded through mining, trade, and agriculture supported his vision to build many structures and monuments in different parts of ancient Egypt. He built thousands of statues that are still full of life to this day, and some might say Ramesses II amplified Amenhotep III's love for statues and gigantic monuments. Also, the Luxor Temple is believed to have been built by Amenhotep III and added more beauty to the temple complex at Karnak. He was particularly famous for his legacy of stone scarabs and tablets that were used for communication. The scarab beetle was a sacred symbol to ancient Egyptians that was linked to the deity Khapre, the god of the rising sun, who was represented in the form of a scarab beetle. Ancient Egyptians believed the scarab was divine due to its ability to appear from beneath the ground. Amenhotep III circulated 200 scarabs made from soapstone across ancient Egypt with each stone documenting different events that happened during his reign. Many scarab stones were made to aid domestic and foreign political correspondence during his reign, and they were also used as religious symbols for different purposes by the people who were alive. He had nine children, including one of his controversial successors who was known as "the heretic."

Tutankhamun

The reign of the pharaoh Tutankhamun, famously known as "King Tut" or the "boy-king," was not long, which was sad for a promising king who ascended to the throne at the age of nine. The reign of King Tut and the king himself are surrounded by many unresolved mysteries and questions. The little that is known about his reign is in the meager details of some of his deeds as a king with a generous heart and great love for his people. He was probably one of the ten children of the "heretic king" Akhenaten and Queen Nefertiti. When he ascended to the throne, he was quick to take a different path from Akhenaten who had chosen to create a new religious system that he promoted by erasing traces of what had been the tradition in ancient Egypt until that point: the worship of many gods and the supreme god, Amun. Instead of Amun and the many other gods, Akhenaten declared an ideological war against the high priests of Amun and commanded the people of ancient Egypt to only worship the Sun disc, Aten. He also moved the religious capital from Thebes to Amarna. There are people who believe Akhenaten may have instituted those religious reforms to significantly reduce the intimidating power of the high priests of Amun. Whatever may have been his reasons for challenging the traditional beliefs of the ancient Egyptians, he paid dearly for it when he died as his reign was removed from the records of the pharaohs who ruled Egypt for about 3,000 years before the details of his radical reforms were found on a clay tablet known as the "Amarna Letters" in 1887.

Perhaps to avoid a similar end, King Tut quickly changed his name from Tutankhaten to Tutankhamun and reversed his father's radical policies and reforms. During his reign between 1332 B.C.E. and 1323 B.C.E. King Tut gave religious power back to the high priests of Amun and promoted the worship of many gods again, according to the tradition in ancient Egypt. He is believed to have also paid the laborers who worked assiduously during the reopening of the temple complexes at Karnak and Luxor from his personal funds. There are Egyptologists who believe King Tut's reversal of his father's radical reforms may have been the result of a massive political pressure from the young king's advisers and members of the nobility who were loyal to the high priests of Amun. At the same time, the most interesting thing about Tutankhamun that shot him into worldwide fame is not the details of his little-known reign but the treasures found in his sealed tomb, which was neither damaged nor raided by tomb robbers. When British archeologist Howard Carter found King Tut's tomb in 1922, it quickly became a global center of attraction due to the thousands of beautiful and rich treasures found in it. There are many theories on how the boy-king died, including that he was poisoned, violently attacked and killed, and died from natural causes due largely to his physical disability. No one is really sure which is true, but the boy-king died very early at just 19 years old.

Xerxes I

Born Kyshayarsa in 520 B.C.E. as a Persian who would later become the king of the Achaemenid Empire in 486 B.C.E., King Xerxes I was one of the rulers of the Twenty-Seventh Dynasty of the Late Period. Also known as Xerxes the Great, he was the son of Darius I and was a favorite son of his parents. He was also a king who believed very much in warfare and military campaigns. When Darius the Great quelled an uprising by the Egyptians in 521 B.C.E. and became the new Persian ruler of Egypt, he showed respect and devotion to the gods and traditions of the ancient Egyptians and let many of the local leaders maintain their power as long as they stayed loyal. The satrapy was the system of administration used by the Persians after they conquered ancient Egypt in 525 B.C.E. under the command of their king, Cambyses. When Xerxes I became the ruler of Egypt, he had little regard for Egyptian religion and tradition, and he waged a serious war against the local rebels causing trouble in Egypt since the days of his father's reign. It was a very challenging campaign, but he eventually won. Also, a lot of his resources went into attacking and conquering Babylonia, and he basically ruled Egypt by proxy. He was rarely in Egypt and mostly ruled through the satrapies, although he did make sure that Egypt continued to pay tributes to the Persian Empire, which were used to fund his military campaigns against Babylonia and his later campaign against Greece.

Xerxes I destroyed the cherished statues of the supreme god of Babylonia, Marduk, and pretty much declared himself the enemy of the Egyptian gods, too. The attempts to conquer Greece made Xerxes I popular and unpopular at the same time. Greek writers and historians never spared an ink to paint him as a mad brutal tyrant from hell. In movies, he was painted pretty much the same and has continued in folk stories to be nothing but a tyrant; however, it is likely that Xerxes I waged a war against the Greeks because he was excessively encouraged and pressured to do so. This theory can be found in records explaining the Persian war against ancient Babylon and the role of Xerxes I during and after the military campaign. Before he launched the campaign against Greece, he prepared extensively for it, but as fate would have it, he did not succeed in that regard, although he recorded some temporary wins during the campaign. When he returned to Persia, he continued to rule Egypt through the satrapies. He could not make much of his reign after the war against the Greeks, although he built some structures and could not finish some. He was eventually assassinated after a period of little to no exploits in power. The later part of his reign and death is believed by historians to be the beginning of the end of the Achaemenid Dynasty in Persia.

Akhenaten

Pharaoh Akhenaten, also known as Akhenaton, was the king that should not have been, but because of his older brother's untimely death, he was crowned the next king of ancient Egypt after his father's death. He changed his name from Amenhotep IV to Akhenaten, which meant "Glory for the Sun Disc," in the sixth year of his seventeen years of reign as the leader of the Unified Two Lands. Akhenaten was probably a co-regent with his father, Amenhotep III, until his father's demise. When Akhenaten became pharaoh in 1353 B.C.E., he was concerned about the ever-rising power of the priesthood of Amun. His solution, which is considered by many scholars as the first example of a monotheistic state policy, was to compel the worship of a new god, the sun disc, across the entire state. The sun disc represented the sun rays shining over ancient Egypt and the royal family, protecting them. In Middle Egypt on the eastern bank of the Nile, he found a suitable site and built a new religious and administrative capital called Akhet-Aten, which meant "the Horizon of the Aten." He moved the capital from Thebes to this new capital and built many temples, tombs, palaces, and villas there. The place is now called Amarna, and discoveries of many kinds, particularly in relation to art and architecture, have been made there.

At Akhet-Aten, the monuments built by Akhenaten, such as temples and statues, are believed today to probably be the first examples of realism in art. The artistic creations have been widely praised for their intimidating lifelike effects and colossal form. By his side throughout his reign was his wife, Queen Nefertiti, whose extremely beautiful bust is considered a great example of the exquisite feminine beauty of the New Kingdom. The queen was the daughter of Ay, the vizier of Amenhotep III. At Akhet-Aten, Akhenaten encouraged what is today known as the art of Amarna. The art form was an impressive progress from what was the norm in art in ancient Egypt until that time, and it had a long-term impact on even the literature and architecture of the time. For example, the statue of Akhenaten is considered an unprecedented representation of the pharaoh, with his projecting lower jaw, fat lips, feminine face, and slim body. The same style of Amarna art was used to depict the other members of the royal family.

Throughout his radical reforms, Akhenaten had the undying love and support of his wife, Queen Nefertiti. Akhenaten also fought multiple battles, and in addition to this, his reign was affected by a severe plague that the priesthood weaponized as the anger of the traditional gods against a "heretic" king. Sadly, the three daughters of Akhenaten and Nefertiti, among a total of ten children, died before their father. Akhenaten died in 1336 B.C.E. at the age of 32, and a significant number of the extensive buildings he commissioned during his lifetime were deliberately destroyed. The new capital city Akhet-Aten was itself significantly reduced to rubble, and the capital was returned to Thebes.

Thutmose III

The reign of Thutmose III in the Eighteenth Dynasty was very crucial to the solidification of the New Kingdom and Egyptian civilization after the chaos of the Second Intermediate Period. His father was Thutmose II, and his mother was one of the lesser wives of the pharaoh. His reign began in 1479 B.C.E. after the death of his aunt and stepmother, Queen Hatshepsut. During Queen Hatshepsut's reign, some battles were fought and won, and new territories were added to ancient Egypt, including parts of Nubia in Southern Egypt. Growing up, Thutmose III focused on his education and developing his military and combat skills, particularly horsemanship and archery. Eventually, he became so good at winning battles that when he became pharaoh he was named the "Warrior King." His reign was a period of extensive military campaigns that aimed to free ancient Egypt from the problems caused by its aggressive neighbors and foreign enemies, including Nubia, Syria, and the Canaanites.

Regarded by his court, the nobility, and all of ancient Egypt as a strong, powerful ruler to be feared, Thutmose III proved them right by fighting many battles and never losing one. Part of his dozens of military campaigns ensured he brought all of Syria under Egyptian control, significantly weakened Nubia (some Egyptologists even say he brought Upper Nubia and Lower Nubia completely under the control of Egypt), and drove back the Mitanni forces in the Euphrates and enemy forces in Sudan. To consolidate territories won, he built fortresses and garrisons and established the office of the "Overseer of Foreign Lands" which deployed qualified individuals to act as the representatives of ancient Egypt in foreign territories and vassal states. In addition to his military achievements, he also instituted economic reforms and built monuments across several Egyptian territories, including the conquered areas. During his reign, the subsequent economic focus of pharaohs on the gold mines was begun and expanded. He also built temples for the Egyptian god Amun at Heliopolis and many other temples for other gods in places such as Amant, Hermopolis, and Kom Ombo.

There are debates among Egyptologists on the nature of the relationship between Hatshepsut and Thutmose III. Although some surviving evidence suggests that Hatshepsut cared very much for the young warrior king, the debates about their relationship arise from the fact that Thutmose III deliberately removed the details of her reign and any signs that suggest she ever reigned from most of the records. For this reason, some Egyptologists have argued that she was probably an overbearing woman who deprived the young Thutmose of his rights as a royal and pharaoh, but others have also argued that Thutmose's military skills and education were the direct results of Hatshepsut's genuine love for the warrior king. In some records, it is said that Hatshepsut may even have trusted Thutmose III with some military responsibilities, although she was generally not disposed to prolonged and extensive military campaigns. For the military exploits and cultural and economic achievements that happened during his reign, Thutmose III was showered with great devotion and respect by the people. He fathered eight children, including Amenhotep II, and his reign lasted for more than 50 years.

Hatshepsut

Thutmose I was the father of Hatshepsut, and when he died, she married her half-brother, Thutmose II. The reign of Queen Hatshepsut began after the death of Thutmose II. Although the heir to the throne was Thutmose III, at 2 years old he was simply too young to carry out his royal duties. As a result, Hatshepsut became the co-regent to the young king and later, to consolidate her position as a pharaoh in her own right, began to assume the responsibilities of a pharaoh.

In the early days, she led a very short military campaign into parts of Nubia and won. She also got the conquered territories to send tributes to ancient Egypt. At the same time, she tried to show that she cared for the young Thutmose III. Some of her early monuments did bear his name as "a partner king," although when the time came to transfer power to him, she did not. Also, there was some resistance in those early days among the patriarchal and conservative nobility. To appease them, she began to dress more as a male king, wearing the royal robes of a pharaoh and sometimes attaching false beards to her chin. Early paintings of her in those days also portrayed her as a male king. Around the sixth year of Thutmose III's reign, she took on the full royal titulary of a pharaoh and started to rule as a female pharaoh. By this time, she had won the support of Hapuseneb, the High Priest of Amun who was greatly respected by the nobility and the people. She also brought a horde of loyalists into her government and ensured they got influential positions in court, including Senenmut who was her architect and held several positions in her government.

Some accounts suggest that Senenmut may have been Hatshepsut's lover, although it is also possible that some people in the patriarchal society in which she found herself were just trying to stain her name. To further consolidate her position, she spread the story that she had been ordained by the chief god of ancient Egypt, Amun, and was a female form of the traditionally male Amun and Horus. Meanwhile, she threw herself into the work of taking the New Kingdom and ancient Egypt to great heights. During her peaceful reign between 1479 B.C.E. and 1459 B.C.E., Hatshepsut entered into trade agreements with foreign states and established trading networks beyond Egypt. She made brief expeditions to the Land of Punt where she promoted the commercial interests of ancient Egypt and returned with many articles of commercial value, including gold and animal skins. In addition, she built monuments and temples on the west and east banks of the Nile. These include her mortuary complex at Luxor where she built her Deir el-Bahari temple, also known as "splendor of splendors," which is now very famous among tourists in Egypt. Due to her many achievements, the fact that she was a female did not become much of an issue for the rest of her 20 years of peaceful and prosperous reign. She had a daughter named Neferure. Neferure was her first and only child.

Chapter 4:

Ramesses II

Ramesses Usermaatre-Setepenre, fondly known as "Sese" among ancient Egyptians, had tremendous respect for his father and his commitment to his military and architectural goals. Ramesses II and his father's love for each other won him the privilege of being a co-regent in the seventh year of his father's reign. As a teenager, Ramesses II dedicated himself to mastering military skills and tactics, like his father Seti I, grandfather Ramesses I, and great-grandfather Seti. "Crown him as king," said Seti I, "that I may see his beauty while I live with him." When Ramesses II proved himself to his father as a young warrior with great potential, he was taken to different military campaigns alongside his father, including a campaign in Libya where he fought excellently despite being a teenager. Later, he would join the Egyptian army's military campaigns to the Palestinian and Mediterranean regions. At the age of 22, alongside two of his sons, Ramesses led a campaign to Nubia and returned to Egypt victorious. During the reign of his father, he cultivated his love for structures and monuments like his father, and in the eastern region of the Nile Delta, Ramesses II and his father built a royal palace at Pi-Ramesses, which Ramesses I had designated as the new capital of Egypt. When he became pharaoh, Ramesses II expanded the royal palace at Pi-Ramesses by attaching chambers and throne rooms, as well as doorways and other important additions to the remarkable sanctuary.

As a pharaoh and military commander, Ramesses the Great focused his attention on securing the borders of ancient Egypt and expanding the territory of his empire. Egypt had many enemies, and Sese understood what was at stake and the importance of taking care of the soldiers and keeping them loyal. Sometimes he formed alliances to secure Egypt from adversaries, as he did when he needed to push back the Assyrians and the Sea Peoples who constantly invaded Egypt in the Thirteenth century B.C.E. Other pirate groups such as the Sherden were subdued by Ramesses the Great, although he was impressed by some of the Sherden pirates whom he employed as bodyguards while he sent the rest of them to the Egyptian army. Sese rewarded his soldiers bountifully and promoted them constantly, just as he did with his courtiers and assistants. During his long campaign against the Hittites, particularly during the Battle of Kadesh, Ramesses II displayed his genius as a strategist and international relations expert. He mobilized a dozen or more allies and divided the entire army into multiple strategic divisions named after different Egyptian gods, part of which about 20,000 Egyptian forces dominated (Lloyd, 2014).

It is estimated that roughly 3,500 Hittite chariots were defeated or pushed back across the River Orontes by Ramesses II and his allies during the battle. When they advanced deep into enemy territory with consistent attacks that helped him secure strategic parts of the Hittite Empire, the king of the Hittites asked for peace. This marked the beginning of what would become "the first peace treaty in the history of the world that was formed on the basis of parity. That is to say, it was made between two equal states" (Lloyd, 2014). Scholars and Egyptologists are not always in agreement as to why Ramesses agreed to the Hittite king's request for peace talks, but one opinion holds that "despite twenty-thousand foot-soldiers, archers, Sherden mercenaries, chariot warriors, and the nick-of-time arrival of yet another division of elite warriors, he did not have enough troops to defeat Muwatallis" (Lloyd, 2014). The peace treaty between the Egyptian and Hittite Empires has been summarized in the following manner (Lloyd, 2014):

> The most important aspect of the treaty was concerned with the treatment of prisoners of war and the return of those who had deserted to the other side. It does not deal with questions about the frontier between the two powers. The contract was sealed by a diplomatic wedding between Ramesses and a daughter of Hattusili III, the Hittite king, but the marriage requested by Hattusili for himself to an Egyptian princess did not take place. (p. 117)

Iconographic evidence from that era also suggests that Ramesses the Great, like the rulers before him, celebrated his military victories with lavish feasts as was the tradition in ancient Egypt. It is believed that these feasts were held by the pharaohs during good times and bad times. To make sure that those who built his many structures across the length and breadth of ancient Egypt were well taken care of, Sese built impressive infrastructures in a village known as Deir el-Medina where skilled workers who worked at the Valley of the Tombs of the Kings lived. The Valley of the Kings was where the majority of the pharaohs of the Eighteenth to Twentieth dynasties were buried. At Northern Abydos where the Osiris Temple (also known as the Terrace of the Great God) is located, one of the most important structures of Ramesses II known as the Portal Temple has continued to be a subject of great interest and intrigue, mainly for its multiple functions culturally, architecturally, and spiritually. The temple was built at a strategic point that intersects with a route that passed through the Osiris Temple, a thoroughfare that served as the processional route for the cult of Osiris, the path to the southern and middle sections of the Abydos necropolis.

To Ramesses II, the Portal Temple was spiritually considered a sacred place where he could maintain close proximity to Osiris and be in the god's favor forever. Festivals and sacred ceremonies were constantly performed at the site in honor of Osiris. Culturally, the Portal Temple has continued to be a wonderful example of storytelling in the New Kingdom, with captivating stories of the reign of the different pharaohs of that time, particularly the reign of Sese. On the exterior walls of the temple, Sese recreated scenes of the usual activities of ancient Egyptians and his reign. Like his father Seti I, Ramesses II inscribed a king list on the walls for future generations, but what was left of it was sold by the French to the British Museum centuries later. There are also scenes showing Ramesses II at the Battle of Kadesh—an extensively documented pitched battle with more than 5,000 chariots between ancient Egypt and the Hittites—as the pharaoh crushed his enemies at the same time. In addition, the temple walls had portrayals of the priests of ancient Egypt, the soldiers and chariots of Ramesses II, the procession of the cult of Osiris, the animals used for sacred ceremonies and sacrifices, royals, nobles, traders, spectators, war prisoners, and so much more. Before 1258 B.C.E. when the Egyptian empire under Ramesses II signed a peace treaty with the Hittite Empire, the Great Hypostyle Hall at Karnak had become a giant monument for historical, political, and cultural advancements in thirteenth century B.C.E. ancient Egypt. For Ramesses II, the Great Hypostyle Hall was a magnificent work that his father had started and that he had to complete. On different sides of the 5,000 sq meter hall are rows and rows of over 130 stone columns and dozens of other giant columns. The sandstone columns were inscribed with the name of Ramesses the Great, and the larger structure was inscribed with his achievements. During his reign, his name and mark were stamped on most of the important structures, especially the temples and royal palaces in various parts of ancient Egypt.

All over Egypt, in parts of Nubia, and several conquered territories, Sese built statues of himself. Also, to celebrate his many achievements, ancient Egyptians made him a god and built statues in his honor both before and after his death. Ramesses the Great was often portrayed as a strong king and a living god—an incarnation of Re who came to life through the vessels of Re, otherwise known as his parents—who was immune to the weaknesses of humans and the human body; although, like everyone else, there were times when his body gave in to the demands of nature. Studies of his mummy have revealed that he dealt with some serious bouts of sickness, including smallpox. As he grew older, his bones and muscles got weaker, and he was seriously affected by arteriosclerosis (hardening of the arteries). Unfortunately, bouts of illnesses were also common among the young, including princes and children of the nobles. Sese lost 12 of his children to such tragedies, and he followed in the footsteps of his predecessors in taking the necessary precautions. This means that the crown prince, the "lesser princes," and sometimes the sons of the nobles were given the same education, as well as the same religious and military training. Because of this practice, the process produced many qualified people who were then assigned different responsibilities as the king deemed fit. According to one account, these "lesser princes" and the sons of the upper-class people got assigned to "positions in the priesthood, while others commanded armies, or became famous architects or administrators. Others no doubt busied themselves with the management of their father's funerary cult and estates, as did the progeny of many wealthy nobles" (Lloyd, 2014). In a specially adorned tomb in the Valley of the Kings at Thebes, the son and successor of Ramesses the Great, Merenptah, laid his father to rest after his death.

Chapter 5:

Amenhotep III

The ancient Egyptian Empire under Amenhotep III, also known as Amana-Hatpa or Amunhotep II, stretched from northern Sudan to the Euphrates. He was born circa 1401 B.C.E. into one of the greatest lineages in ancient Egypt, the Thutmosid line, which had been in power for about 150 years. A great and wealthy king, Amenhotep III was revered by the royals, his court, and friends in several parts of the world for his diplomacy, leadership, and other skills. He was a generous king, and his kindness endeared him to rulers in other parts of the world. It is believed that a Mitanni king, King Shutama or Shuttarna II, who was possibly a maternal relative of Amenhotep III, sent gifts to Amenhotep III from time to time. At one point, the Mittani king sent a Mitanni princess, Gilukhipa, with an entourage of hundreds of Mitannis to Amenhotep III for marriage. However, Amana-Hatpa never sent any Egyptian woman abroad, which was in line with the long-time tradition of the pharaohs before him. He continued on the path of the Eighteenth Dynasty kings before him, solidified their achievements internally and externally, and made sure vassal states such as Amurru (part of modern Syria), Nubia, and other territories conquered by his predecessors sent their tributes regularly.

Three things made the 38-year reign of Amenhotep III remarkable: the abiding peace throughout his reign, the promotion and growth of artistic innovations and great architectural works, and the incredible economic and political advancements. Although his reign was mostly peaceful and the powerful Egyptian military was always quick to crush any rebellions, there is an account of a very short campaign to Nubia in the fifth year of Amenhotep III's reign for which the pharaoh was described as a "mighty bull, strong in might...the fierce-eyed lion" (Clayton, 1994). He also devoted his time to large-scale construction all over Egypt—thanks to the huge amount of profit made from trade and other commercial activities—and he made sure that temples and monuments in honor of different ancient Egyptian gods were in abundance. He thought of himself as "the one who brings plans into existence, abundant in monuments, plentiful in miracles" (Snape, 2021). True to his description of himself, he built a copious number of monuments for himself, including his two colossal statues known as the Colossi of Memnon, which was named by the Greeks after the Ethiopian King and Trojan hero, Memnon, who was killed by Achilles in Greek Mythology. Apart from the fact that the Colossi of Memnon were part of the mortuary complex of Amenhotep III, one of the things that captivated the ancient Egyptians was that after an earthquake created big cracks on the statues in 1200 B.C.E., one of the statues would sometimes "sing" at dawn. The high-pitched sound made by the statue was believed to be a divine blessing by many ancient Egyptians, and it remained so down to the time of the Romans when Septimius Severus, a Roman Emperor in the third century B.C.E., ordered the destroyed parts of the statue to be patched up. The repair was done badly and the "singing" stopped as a result.

To make life easier for the people, Amenhotep III built infrastructures throughout Egypt, including public relaxation spots for artisans and the general public. In the Eastern Desert on the eastern part of the Nile, a massive amount of gold was mined in the mines at Wadi Hammamat and used to increase the economic standing of the Egyptian Empire. In addition, the Khaemhet, the official office for grain in ancient Egypt, celebrated bountiful grain harvests. In the 30th year of his reign, the plentiful harvests were especially celebrated. Under his reign, Amenhotep III brought the people closer to Khepri and popularized the role of the morning sun god by associating the god with royal missives, particularly the scarabs. He also promoted the worship of the solar god Aten and built the sun court, an open courtyard space at Luxor Temple, for unfettered access to the divine power of Aten. In the place of the kings before him, it is believed that Amenhotep III identified with the deities and the solar god, especially because "his buildings document an unparalleled emphasis on solar theology, such that the cults of Nekhbet, Amun, Thoth, and Horus-khenty-khenty, were heavily solarized" (Shaw, 2003). Some scholars have argued that Amenhotep III promoted several gods during his reign to "curb the growing power of the priesthood of Amun," (Clayton, 1994) although his son, Akhenaten, took it more than a step further. Amenhotep III's love for encouraging many forms of art when it came to building statues and sculptural works gave his reign its own uniqueness. The life-sized and other types of statues made during his reign were created with human and animal representations that led to associations of Amenhotep III with several Egyptian gods. In fact, Amenhotep III was worshiped as a god both in Egypt and in Nubia where he had a cult temple for people to worship him. In the temple that Amenhotep III built for Amun on the eastern part of the Luxor Temple, the story of his birth is told in special reliefs designed to captivate the reader. Clayton (1994) has explained the reliefs in the following manner:

> The creator god, the ram-headed Khnum of Elephantine, is seen fashioning the young king and his *ka* (spirit double) on a potter's wheel, watched by the goddess Isis. The god Amun is then led to his meeting with the queen by his ibis-headed Thoth, god of wisdom. Subsequently, Amun is shown standing in the presence of the goddess Hathor and Mut nursing the child created by Khnum. (p. 115)

Some scholars believe the architectural vision of Amenhotep III focused a lot on "the magnification of royal iconography," which inspired new types of royal family statues, including "striding queen and princess statues, along with standing images of daughters as part of royal family groups" (Lloyd, 2014). The pharaoh's vision also inspired the upper class to "utilize a broad range of types in both tomb and temple settings, including scribal, block, offering, seated, and striding figures" (Lloyd, 2014). Amenhotep III built a palace complex at Malqata, on the opposite side of Waset or Thebes, and beautified the temple of the god Re and the god Amun at Amada in Nubia. At Nubia, he built temples for himself and his highly loved and respected wife, Queen Tiye, as incarnates of the gods, and the people worshiped them. At Soleb, on the western bank of the Nile he directed his architect, Amenhotep son of Hapu, to build his famous Funerary Temple of Amenhotep III, which he named "Mansion of Millions of Years." Long after he married his wife Queen Tiye, who did not descend from a royal line, he created an artificial lake for her in the 11th year of his reign and named it "pleasure lake." Their marriage had been made public in an unusual display of love and royal power. It was probably the most affectionate use of scarabs by Amenhotep III. The scarab inscription had the following words (Mertz, 2009):

May he live, Amenhotep III, given life, and the King's Great Wife Tiye, who lives. The name of her father is Yuya, the name of her mother is Thuya; she is the wife of a mighty king whose southern boundary is as far as Karoy, and northern as far as Naharin! (p. 242)

Queen Tiye's father Yuya, who was also the Commander of Chariots during Amenhotep III's reign, was buried in a tomb that was partly covered in golden chariots with beautiful leatherwork that suggests the glory of the era. Pharaoh Amana-Hatpa also built temples and statues for his wife to be worshiped as a supernatural being. Together, they produced nine children, two of whom Amenhotep III married and gave the title of Great Royal Wife in the last decade of his reign.

Amenhotep III was said to have spent time regularly in a palace at Thebes where his lesser wives and the majority of the wives sent by his allies and friends lived. On several occasions, Amenhotep III left state duties and sometimes international responsibilities to Queen Tiye and the court. However, he also expanded the temple of Amen-Ra at Karnak and built other temples that were as remarkable in size and design, including the temple he built for the husband of Sekhmet, Ptah. There were over 700 statues of the lioness-goddess Sekhmet made during his reign, although what is left is not as many now. The statues were mostly used during sacred ceremonies and sacrifices for the protection of the king and the people and the recovery of the sick. As he grew older, Amenhotep III became obese and developed a tooth problem, which severely affected him. It was so bad that one of his "brother" kings, the King of Babylon or King Tushratta, sent him a statue of the goddess of healing in Babylon, Ishtar, hoping he would get well quickly. At about the age of 45, Amenhotep III gave up the ghost and was buried in a tomb that is widely believed to have been originally meant for his father, Tuthmosis IV. He was succeeded by his son Akhenaten, and his wife, Queen Tiye, may have lived to be 54 or 57 years old before she died.

Chapter 6:

Tutankhamun

Born in Amarna to Pharaoh Akhenaten and Queen Nefertiti, Tutankhamun ("Living Image of Amun") was initially named Tutankhaten, in line with his father's radical religious reforms and promotion of the strict monotheistic cult of Aten. It was after he ascended the throne, possibly in his second regnal year, that he changed his name to Tutankhamun and the name of his wife and half-sister from Ankhesenpaaten to Queen Ankhesenamen, promoting once again Amun as the chief god of ancient Egyptians. Also, when he moved the seat of government from Amarna to Thebes and restored the names of monuments to their original deity names after they had been radically changed from Amun to Aten, he revoked his father's actions, and he announced his intention to work with the nobles and prescribed priests of Amun to promote religious diversity and stability again in the state. His main advisors were his stepmother (before her death), Queen Nefertiti, his grandfather Ay, and the same Amarna court officials that served his father, Akhenaten, which tells us a lot about the advanced nature of politics in ancient Egypt.

Among the top officials advising King Tut were Horemhab and Ay. Horemhab, a top military official, was one of the people who openly disagreed with Akhenaten's radical reforms, and it is said among some scholars that he refused to move to Amarna in protest against the king's decision to enforce the worship of the solar god. When King Tut ascended to the throne, he was quick to advise, by virtue of his government position and the crisis that followed Akhenaten's death, that the capital should be moved back to Thebes. In his famous Restoration Stela where he explained the reasons why he was revoking his father's actions and restoring Amun as the chief god of ancient Egypt, the anger of the gods that Akhenaten rejected was believed to have caused misfortune for Egypt. According to Shaw (2003):

The temples of the gods had become ruins, their cults abolished. The gods had, therefore, abandoned Egypt; if one prayed to them, they no longer answered, and, when the army was sent to Syria to expand the boundaries of Egypt, it met with no success. The prominence of this last phrase probably indicates why the army no longer supported Amarna policy. (p. 347)

To appease the gods, King Tut commissioned a long list of restoration and reinstallation programs. One account has observed that "His Majesty made monuments for the gods...building their shrines anew" (Snape, 2021). At the same time, Tutankhamun built temples for himself in Faras and Kawa in Nubia just like he did for the restored gods all over Egypt, and he encouraged cult worship of his name and status. During his nine-year reign, he spent greatly on building artistic structures all over Egypt. It has been noted that "extensive building works were carried out at Karnak and Luxor in Tutankhamun's name, especially the great colonnade and the relief scenes of the Festival of Opet at Luxor, but all were subsequently taken over by Horemheb" (Clayton, 1994). He saw himself as "the one who built the one who built him, who fashioned the one who fashioned him," (Lloyd, 2014) promoting the not-so-unusual view that he was one and the same with the gods, and the gods were one and the same with him. In his unusually small tomb, also known as KV 62 (King's Valley 62) in the Valley of the Kings, Egyptologists found treasures that revealed the hobbies of the boy king and the affluent life that he lived. A golden hand fan buried in his grave shows how much King Tut loved hunting ostriches, and a statuette of Serqet (the goddess of the dead and infinite dark waters), a throne, a funerary mask, and a knife sheath, all made of gold, confirm how much he, like many of his predecessors, cherished anything made of gold both in life and in death.

Apart from the fact that the ancient Egyptian Empire in the New Kingdom was at the apex of its gold-producing capacity and was unrivaled by other states, the tradition of burying the pharaohs with expensive grave goods, particularly gold, has been interpreted as a sign of wisdom on the part of the pharaohs. It has been noted that during this period, "royal and upper-class burial customs had the effect of operating as compulsory saving, 'trapping' large quantities of gold in tombs, and so keeping it out of circulation" (Johnson, 2012). A model coffin was also found in KV 62 in which the young king preserved his grandmother's hair lock, a sign that he had a great love for his family and was probably very attached to his grandmother, Queen Tiye. A canopic chest with four jars containing his internal organs was also found in his tomb. Queen Ankhesenamen outlived King Tut, even though she was five years older than him. They did not have any children together; she is believed to have given birth to two stillborn babies that were buried with King Tut in his tomb. When King Tut died without an heir at the age of 19, there was a crisis in Egypt that put Queen Ankhesenamen in a difficult position. She tried to take the throne for herself by writing to the king of the Hittites at the time to send one of his sons to marry her and become the next king of Egypt. It was a strange proposal to make given the history between the two powers.

The Hittite king agreed to her proposal and sent one of his sons who was killed before he could enter Egypt. The death of the prince put the Queen in a more difficult position and made the crisis in Egypt, as well as the animosity between Egypt and the Hittites, worse. She would later marry Ay, probably her grandfather and also a senior member of the court under King Tut's reign, who ruled Egypt for about three years before his death. His death led to a military capture of the throne by Horemhab, the man who was known as the King's Deputy during the reign of King Tut. The position of the King's Deputy was a powerful one that put Horemhab, a complete military man, in a position to seize the throne after Ay died. It is also possible that Horemhab became the King's Deputy after the death of Queen Nefertiti early in King Tut's short reign. In simple terms, we can also call Horemhab a regent, although he was not of royal birth, but he became regent mostly because of his status as a military commander. During the reign of King Tut, Horemhab was very likely the man who led the military campaigns, as he is believed to have been on one of those campaigns when Ay became the king. According to Clayton (1994):

> Military campaigns were apparently mounted in Nubia and Palestine/Syria, suggested by a brightly painted gesso box from Tutankhamun's tomb which has four spirited scenes featuring the king. One shows him hunting lions in the desert, another gazelles, whilst on the third and fourth he furiously attacks

Nubians and then Syrians, who fall to his arrows. Finely carved scenes of prisoners in the Memphite tomb of the military commander-in-chief, Horemheb, lend some veracity to the scenes on the gesso box, as does the painting in the tomb of Huy, Viceroy of Nubia, which shows subservient Nubian princes and piles of tribute. It is doubtful, however, that Tutankhamun actually took part in any of the campaigns. (p. 130)

Horemhab would probably have seized the throne after the death of King Tut had he not been in Hittite on a campaign. One of his tombs describes him as a military commander who was "renowned in the land of the Hittites," (Shaw, 2003) and since the Hittites were a constant enemy of Egypt, it is not difficult to understand that Horemhab's renown was due to his fierce military abilities. Also, Horemhab was the one who ordered the demolition of Amarna as well as the statues and anything that can be traced to the reign of Akhenaten, including his original burial site and remains. The demolition plan would have affected the tomb of King Tut as well, but due to a very important intervention, the disaster was prevented. It is believed that a court official named Maya, who served under the reign of King Tut and Horemhab as the head of the treasury department, saved the tomb of Tutankhamun from destruction and looting and moved the mummy of Akhenaten as well. The fact that Maya's intervention helped to preserve the treasures in Tutankhamun's tomb was a remarkable feat, especially when we consider how intense the looting of royal tombs was at the time. According to Johnson (2012), the looting of royal tombs was so bad that a weary observation—presumably by a royal or upper-class official—was made in the New Kingdom that:

> They who built with granite, who set a hall inside their pyramid, and wrought beauty with their fine work...their altar stones also are empty as are those of the weary ones, the ones who die by the riverside leaving no mourners. (p. 217)

In spite of Maya's intervention, the names of Akhenaten, Smenkhkare, Tutankhamun, and Ay were removed from the Karnak and Abydos's King Lists, possibly in line with the command of Horemhab. Horemhab built two tombs for himself, one while he was just a military commander and another while he was a pharaoh. Following his reign of between 14 to 27 years as a military ruler, Horemhab died and so did the Eighteenth Dynasty with him.

Chapter 7:

Khufu

For more than 4,000 years, the reign of Khufu (also known as Cheops or Suphis) in the Fourth Dynasty has remained one of the most unforgettable reigns of any Egyptian pharaoh. Born Khnum-Khufu ("Khnum Protects Me") in the Old Kingdom in a province called Menat-Khufu, Khufu grew up in a big family, and his siblings included Rahotep, Ankhhaf, Kanefer, Meritites, Henutsen, among others. Apart from Queen Meritites I and Queen Henutsen, his sisters whom he married, Khufu also had a third wife whose name is not known but is believed to have given birth to Redjedef or Djedefre, the pharaoh who succeeded Khufu. Among his other children, Khufu also fathered Khafre, Kawab, Baufre, Hordjedef or Djedhefor, all males, as well as Hetepheres II, Meresankh II, Nefertiabet, Khamerernebty I, and Meritites II, who were some of his daughters. As the second pharaoh of the Fourth Dynasty, archeologists, Egyptologists, and historians are yet to gather the details of his reign over a united Upper and Lower Egypt. However, one major discovery that has assured us that Khufu truly existed is his ivory figurine, a very small statuette that is less than one meter in height. Originally, the figurine was found without the head by the famous British archeologist, William Flinders Petrie, who is often called the father of Egyptology. It would take three additional weeks before the head was found and reattached to the figurine in 1903. Some scholars believe that the figurine was probably a votive offering, which made it an exception to Khufu's *likely* general ban on the erection of any statue in his image.

When it came to building pyramids, Khufu achieved a revolutionary feat by dreaming of "Akhet Khufu," which means "the Horizon of Khufu," and brought it to life in a way that has continued to be a marvel to the world today. Among Khufu's state officials, many of them being his relatives, there was Hemiunu or Hemon, a nephew of Khufu whose responsibility it was to be in charge of the building of the

Great Pyramid at Giza, and other important tasks regarding royal tombs and tomb design, particularly that of King Khufu's mother, Queen Hetepheres I. Hemiunu was simply the principal architect of any building project during Khufu's reign; his mastaba was built close to the Great Pyramid. In a way, the tendency to build innovative pyramid structures can be said to be a family trait of the Fourth Dynasty lineage, starting from Sneferu to Khufu, Khafre and Menkaure, although none was as impressive as Khufu's. It took about 20 years to erect the Great Pyramid of Giza, the only standing monument out of the Seven Wonders of the Ancient World. An excellent example of the remarkable wisdom of ancient Egyptians, the builders of Khufu's Great Pyramid left behind a great mystery as to how the massive monument was built. There has been no convincing theory in the modern world on how exactly the Great Pyramid was built. For Shaw (2003), the Great Pyramid's "enormous size, the astonishing mathematical properties of its design, and the perfection and accuracy of its construction still invite unscientific explanations." Apart from its intimidating height and the mastabas for royals and nobles that were built very close to the monument, the Great Pyramid itself includes the King's chamber where Khufu's sarcophagus is located, an unfinished underground chamber, a closed corridor to the south, and a mortuary temple to the east, which is linked to a causeway that leads to the valley temple. The Great Pyramid project was a symbol of grand political, cultural, and economic statements in the ancient world.

From an economic standpoint, Khufu's monument is believed to have "considerably revitalized the economy and society, with unprecedented use of raw materials coming from the margins of the Valley (white limestone from Tura, basalt from the North Fayum, alabaster from Hatnub, granodiorite from Aswan)" (Lloyd, 2014). In addition to these, there were also "the copper minerals and malachite from Sinai, the red hematite ochre from Abu Ballas, or gneiss from Lower Nubia, all of which necessitated the setting up of appropriate expeditions and adequate logistics, particularly for the provision of water" (Lloyd, 2014). In many ways, the Great Pyramid is considered to be the perfection of all previous attempts by the kings before Khufu to build something extraordinary, something that represents the journey of ancient Egypt and its culture and society, an example of what the Egypt of that era hoped to become in the future (Romer, 2013). For some scholars, the Great Pyramid is a special example of the unique desire that ancient Egyptian pharaohs had to reach the afterlife and be with the gods. One argument has suggested that the construction of the Great Pyramid was an attempt to solve an age-old problem that the pharaohs dealt with reign after reign: the desire to "project the King's *ka* to the stars, and to retrieve him" (Hitchins, n.d.). Before Khufu's Great Pyramid, some of the earlier suggestions to resolve this problem included "rising on smoke, going up with thunderclouds, climbing a rope to the Great Hitching Post (celestial north pole, the star Thuban at the time)," among others. However, when Khufu decided to build the Great Pyramid, according to Hitchins (n.d.), his goal was likely to use the monument as a kind of "*psychic* machine" through which "daily prayer and offerings by a dedicated priesthood [would become] the power source to project the King's *ka*." In a more detailed explanation, Hitchins (n.d.) has extensively argued that:

> There were several places the King's *ka* would visit, and these are all catered for in the design of *Akhet* Khufu. They also seem to be arranged so that he could travel by day or night. By day, the King would spend his time in the so-called Queen's Chamber, more likely a *serdab* [a secret chamber in a tomb for protecting the *ka* of the deceased] for a missing *ka* statue of the king which would have fitted into the niche built into the East wall of the chamber. From this *serdab*, his *ka* could roam either north or south, so that he could look after his people and maintain Ma'at. Whether he envisaged travel over land and river, or instead over a figurative map of the land and river on top of the Mound of Creation, is moot. There were, after all, several boats buried near the pyramid which he might be able to magically reassemble and use…or not.
>
> By night, he could travel from the King's Chamber to the Southern Netherworld, which was presumed to be in the direction of Al Nitak, the leftmost star in Orion's Belt, which culminated at 45°, matching the slope of the shaft KC(S). Here the King would engage with other gods of the heavens to negotiate a good Inundation for his people of Egypt. Or, the King could travel to the Northern Netherworld, where his stellar palace awaited him, and where he would become an

"akh," a shining one: KC(N) was aimed at the Great Hitching Post.

The King's sarcophagus, containing the mummified King, would then be the power source for all of the travelling, energized daily—and perhaps nightly, too—by priestly prayers, lustrations and offerings.

There have been several controversies built over the years around the building of the Great Pyramid from the system of labor to the funding of the project. One, there is the controversy that Khufu sold one of his princesses into prostitution to fund the construction of the Great Pyramid. This controversial view has been pushed mostly by Greek historians and writers, but it may not be true. Another controversy states that the workers who worked for 20 years building the pyramid were slaves; although other scholars have disputed this claim, with some saying that it was more likely for what we call statute labor—a kind of mandatory, unpaid labor required in a feudal system—to have been the labor system in place at the time. Another account has suggested that the builders of the pyramid may be either conscripted citizens or patriotic citizens who felt a sense of responsibility toward their god-king (Kemp, 2018). For Kemp (2018), the question of how labor was handled for the building of monuments, particularly the extremely difficult monuments such as the Great Pyramid, may be more complicated to answer now because of the many differences between the modern world and the ancient world, particularly in relation to terminology, the system of government, and socio-cultural experiences. When everything concerning labor is considered, whether in relation to laborers as conscripted or patriotic citizens, Kemp (2018) believes we should be more interested in finding out if "the conditions of service were a lot harsher than those of life at home, and whether they were largely resented." To provide an answer to this serious question, the author explains that the answer is more likely to be a system of volunteer labor. Kemp (2018) explains that:

It was based upon the sense of obligation to others higher in the chain of authority (the king at the top) that was instilled in an individual from birth, together with a liking for organizing people into groups each of which was given a name and thus a sense of identity and a basis for bonding. Prominent amongst these groups was the phyle, the same unit used in the organization of temple staff. They took their names from the positions which groups of sailors would occupy when forming the crew of a boat, thus 'starboard,' 'port,' 'bow,' 'stern' and one of uncertain translation. There were both larger and smaller units of organization. The former used the word for a full boat's 'crew.' The names of some of them (such as 'Friends of Khufu') occur daubed in red paint on cut blocks of stone used, for example, in the construction of the pyramids at Giza and on the blocks used to seal the underground storerooms at the Wadi el-Jarf seasonal port on the Red Sea coast. The smaller units, possibly of ten men, took names such as 'strong,' 'first,' 'noble' and 'rising,' The system (or at least the way it expressed itself in writing) developed over time. After the Fourth Dynasty and the building of the Giza pyramids the crews tended to take their names from those of prominent people, not only high officials but king's wives and daughters. Detailed studies have concluded that such crews belonged to these named individuals who were thus donating labour that was under their control to the projects of others. To what extent these crews returned after each assignment to a life based in their own homes, perhaps cultivating their own fields, is not known. (pp. 180-181)

According to a papyrus roll in Berlin known as the Westcar Papyrus (or the Berlin papyri), ancient Egyptians had a collection of stories and fables that were very popular and well circulated during the reign of Khufu. One of the stories, famously known as the story of Khufu and the Magician, paints a picture of the richness of Egyptian myth and their belief in magic and the miracles of their gods. The storyteller is one of the sons of Khufu, Prince Hordedef, who is said to have been telling Khufu about a man named Djedi, a great magician in Egypt. Djedi was said to have the power to find out and disclose the secrets of Egyptian gods, particularly the secret chambers in the temple of Thoth, as well as the power to tame wild animals, make broken things new again, and bring a dead animal back to life. When Khufu heard this, he could not resist the urge to see the famous magician and test his powers. As a result, he issued a royal summons to bring the magician before him. When Djedi arrived at the palace, there were many spectators already waiting, most of them naysayers who were also high-ranking court officials. Khufu, determined to see what the magician could really do, commanded his servants to bring a criminal that had been condemned to execution by beheading, a bullock, a water bird, and a goose. When the king's command was fulfilled, Djedi was commanded to behead the criminal and put the head back on his neck. The magician refused to obey the command as he believed it was a cruel thing to do, but to appease the king, he asked for his permission to behead the goose and put back its head. When he got the king's permission to proceed, he achieved the goal without any difficulty. Everybody was amazed from the court officials to the other spectators. The king was not fully convinced, though, so he asked the old magician to tell him the number of secret chambers in the temple of Thoth.

Again, the magician refused to do as the king commanded, saying he had no such knowledge. Instead, he told the king he had a prophecy that concerned who will rule Egypt after Khufu's death. When Khufu heard this, his interest was piqued, so he asked the magician to tell him the prophecy. The prophecy was linked to the wife of the High Priest of Re, Reweddjedet, who was pregnant at the time. The old magician said the three children of Reweddjedet—Userkaf (Strength is His Soul), Sahure (Feet of Re), and Neferirkare (Beautiful is the Soul of Re)—will be created in the image of the god Re and be the next rulers of Egypt. Khufu was not happy that the prophecy did not name any of his sons as his heir. To make him happy, the old magician suggested a pact between the High Priest of Re and Khufu, which would allow his son Menkaure and grandson Shepseskaf to rule Egypt before the three children of Reweddjedet. Although the end of the story is not known as that part of the papyrus roll has been destroyed, we do know that the Fourth Dynasty ended with the son and grandson of Khufu and the Fifth Dynasty began with the three children of Reweddjedet. Apart from this story, the Berlin papyri also include other stories set in the period of Khufu's reign and cover different informative writings on health and wellbeing, including medical guides on how to diagnose different diseases and health conditions such as infertility, heart health, rheumatism, and more. The great pharaoh himself, Khnum-Khufu, died in a mysterious manner after 23 years on the throne, although there are records and arguments suggesting his reign may have lasted longer, especially when we consider the duration of the construction of the Great Pyramid and other structures during his reign.

Chapter 8:

Hatshepsut (1478 B.C.E.–1458

B.C.E.)

The Queen-Pharaoh Maatkare ("Truth is the Soul of Re"), famously known as Hatshepsut, was the daughter of the Great Royal Wife to Thutmose I, Queen Ahmose I. She had two male siblings, Wadjmose and Amenmose, and one older sister, Neferhukeb, who died at a young age. Her two brothers also died young, long before their father, although it is believed that Amenmose died as an army general. Given that she was the only child of her parents who did not die early, it is probably apt to say Hatshepsut, meaning "Foremost of the Noble Ones," was a perfect name for the woman-pharaoh. Her husband and half-brother, Thutmose II, died between 1476 B.C.E. and 1478 B.C.E. from a chronic illness and left behind a 2-year-old son, Thutmose III, who was the son of a lesser wife. Since the heir to the throne was still a child, Hatshepsut stepped up to the plate to run the country on his behalf until he came of age. She was a very beautiful, highly educated, and glamorous woman who found favor with the priests and the court officials.

To keep the economy thriving, she sent several expeditions to Punt, a very crucial place of economic value to ancient Egyptians. During the reign of Hatshepsut, gold, ivory tusks, electrum, myrrh, perfumes, food spices, and various luxury goods and wares were constantly moved from Punt to Egypt in sailing boats. Sometimes, the expeditions of the Egyptians were not solely for trade purposes; the Egyptian military also voyaged there during the reign of Maatkare. In addition to Punt, Hatshepsut explored the Sinai Peninsula, like many kings before and after her, for valuable stones and minerals from turquoise to copper and many others. Due to the trading expeditions during her reign, ancient Egyptians described her as "the bow-rope of Upper Egypt, the mooring-post of the southerners, the effective stern-rope of Lower Egypt" (Wilkinson, 2014). When the time came for her to solidify her claim to the throne as a god-king, she had reliefs made at the funerary temple she built at Deir el-Bahri that promoted her mother as a young maiden with whom the god Amun was well pleased and slept with under a rain of gold.

In Lower Nubia, on the west bank of the Nile, Hatshepsut built a temple with several sanctuaries on the southern part of the Buhen fortress. It is believed that Hatshepsut sanctioned a number of military expeditions against the enemies of Egypt. She also spent heavily on building projects across northern and southern Egypt, from redecorations to her own exclusive projects that included temples, chapels, and obelisks. These included "the quarrying, transport, and erection of a series of enormous granite obelisks at Karnak, whose inscriptions clarify that their purpose was to honour Amen-Ra" (Snape, 2021). The obelisk was about 96 feet tall. Other building projects were made to honor the gods, particularly Amun, and to show that Hatshepsut had their support in everything she did as Pharaoh. Built in a very crucial spot at Karnak, one of her most notable projects, a shrine famously called the Red Chapel, has different kinds of art portraying powerful spiritual forces, including a scene showing how fire destroyed the effigies of those who were against the reign of Maatkare. Hatshepsut also built a temple at Speos Artemidos—an archeological site that is only a short distance from the Beni Hasan cemetery—for Pehkhet, the Egyptian goddess of war, often depicted as a lioness. According to the inscriptions on the walls of the temple, Hatshepsut (Shaw, 2003) claimed that:

> I have raised up what was dismembered from the first time when the Asiatics were in Avaris of the North Land (with) roving hordes in the midst of them overthrowing what had been made. The Temple of the Lady Cusae was fallen into dissolution, the earth had swallowed up its noble sanctuary, and children danced on its roof. (p. 227)

The above text is believed to be part of a series of royal propaganda to show the strength of Maatkare and her capacity to rule over the land in the strongest possible way whenever the need arose. Although she publicly showed her disapproval of the Asiatics, it is not certain that she ordered or sanctioned any expedition against them. Unlike many male kings with weak authority in power, Hatshepsut had total control during her reign, and her influence spread all over ancient Egypt and beyond. As a matter of fact, an inscription at her temple claims that "[t]he king of the gods, Amun-Re, came forth from his temple saying: 'Welcome my sweet daughter, my favourite, the King of Upper and Lower Egypt, the *maat-lover*, Hatshepsut—thou art the king, take possession of the Two Lands" (Johnson, 2012). Also, one of her statues has an inscription that says "My reward from my father is life, stability, and dominion on the Horus-throne of the Living, like Ra, forever" (Snape, 2021). Although she built herself a tomb at the Valley of the Kings, it has been mostly empty since its construction.

In the early days of her reign as the pharaoh, she had statues made of her looking like a male ruler and a sphinx. Among the court officials that worked for Hatshepsut was Nebwawi, an Osiris priest; Neferkhewet, an architect of the royal family; Thuity, who was the chief supervisor of the royal residence and held multiple titles; Nehesy, the head of the treasury department and chancellor; and A'ametju, who was a loyal vizier during her reign. A'ametju came from a long line of famous viziers in ancient Egypt that included Neferuben, his father who was also a vizier in Lower Egypt, and Userman, his uncle who was a vizier during the reign of Thutmose III. Also, there was Amenemhet IV, who served Hatshepsut like his brother Senenmut. Amenemhet was a temple official during the reign of Maatkare and led many Amun festivals in Thebes. Together with Hapuseneb, the famous and respected prophet of Amun who supported Hatshepsut in many ways, Amenemhet IV frequently led the *hes* cleansing ceremony, also called baptism, that was performed during Hatshepsut's crowning as a legitimate Pharaoh. Reliefs on the walls of her funerary temple at Deir el-Bahri also show her receiving the blessing of her father, Thutmose I, to become the heir to the throne. It is difficult to confirm, outside of what Hatshepsut herself said, that she truly had the support of Thutmose I or that her father showed her to the court as his successor, particularly as the next ruler before Thutmose III. On the walls of Deir el-Bahri, she had it written that Thutmose I had presented her to the court saying (Kemp, 2018):

> This is my daughter, Khnemet-Amun Hatshepsut, may she live. I designate her as my successor. She it is who shall be on this

throne. Assuredly, it is she who shall guide you. Obey her word, assemble you at her command. For she is your god, the daughter of a god. (p. 262)

However, we do know that Hatshepsut knew her father was a strong and well-respected king. She was no stranger to the politics of ancient Egypt, so it would be right to say she took the opportunity to solidify her claim to the throne using his name and reputation. As part of the roles she had to assume when she became Queen-Pharaoh, Maatkare also became a priestess in the temple of Amun and was known as the "God's Wife of Amun," automatically becoming the spiritual leader of all the women serving in Amun's temple. It is believed that Hatshepsut also brought up her daughter, Neferure, in the way of a priestess of Amun's temple, so she could one day become the next God's Wife of Amun Temple. Over the years, her daughter became a respected priestess in the Harem of the Temple of Amun and one of the pillars of Hatshepsut's reign due to her spiritual role in the state. Unfortunately, Neferure died before her mother, and her death came not long before the death of Senenmut, a top official in Hatshepsut's court and possibly her lover. Senenmut was a very important official during the reign of Maatkare; he had many responsibilities in the areas of religion, politics, and education. He was Maatkare's most trusted advisor, a very respected architect, a powerful court official that led the group of influential nobles and priests who supported Hatshepsut, and he was close enough to the Queen-Pharaoh to be the private tutor of Neferure, her only daughter.

An inscription on a statue of Senenmut at Thebes confirms that it was he "who conducted all the works of the king in Karnak, in Armant and Deir el-Bahri; and of Amun in the temple of Mut, in Ishry and in Luxor Temple" (Wilkinson, 2014). At Karnak, it is said that one of Senenmut's projects for Hatshepsut "remains unique, and uniquely impressive, the perfect marriage of natural landscape and man-made edifice" (Wilkinson, 2014). Hatshepsut loved animals and kept different breeds of dogs in her palace that she spent time with regularly. It is not clear whether Hatshepsut gave up the throne voluntarily or died in power, but it is believed that her disappearance happened during one of the crucial military campaigns that Thutmose III went on. Whether she died naturally or was assassinated has not been confirmed.

Chapter 9:

Thutmose III

The warrior king Thutmose III, often praised enthusiastically by ancient Egyptians as the "Life to Horus, Mighty Bull Appearing in Thebes," who achieved many outstanding feats on the fields of battle during his reign, ruled over a vast Egypt that he brought to the zenith of its power, ranging from today's capital of Sudan, Khartoum, to the Euphrates. As the crown prince, he received training in various military skills and strategies, and he also learned the religious ways of ancient Egyptians, especially as an inductee of the "Pillar of His Mother," a religious cult. In the ancient Egyptian caste system, those inducted into the Pillar of His Mother caste were members of an exclusive group of priests, and all prospective members had to be a prince, at the minimum, before they were considered. It is believed that this strict requirement existed because of the seriousness of what the group represented, which was to be the citadel of training future rulers on how to be great defenders of Egypt. The knowledge and experience he gained in the cult and during his military training, especially at the Egyptian naval base, would become useful to him during his campaigns under the reign of Hatshepsut and when he came fully into power after Hatshepsut left the scene.

Thutmose III followed in the footsteps of his grandfather, Thutmose I and conquered an extensive number of territories which he ruled through loyalists that were either from Egypt or were born in a foreign land and trained in Egypt to later return to their land of origin and rule as vassals of Egypt. He also installed many scholars and politicians who were skilled in international politics in the courts of the vassal states to ensure they were kept loyal to Egypt and the warrior king. Although Thutmose III grew up learning military tactics and skills, his life as a warrior king was somehow determined by the political situation that threatened Egypt during his reign. Before the end of the reign of the Queen-Pharaoh, Hatshepsut, the vassals in the territories conquered by his grandfather, Thutmose I, had begun to rebel and refuse to pay their tributes. In the Sinai Peninsula and parts of Palestine, there were growing threats to the economic and political stability of Egypt, and other big powers of the time, such as the Mitannis who had always been threatened by the power of Egypt, had started to form a military coalition against Egypt.

When all the forces against Egypt came together, they presented a united front behind the King of Kadesh and the Prince of Megiddo. Thutmose III set out with an army of between 20,000 to 30,000 men to meet the enemies on the battlefield, which led to the famous Battle of Megiddo where the Egyptian forces forced the enemy coalition into a difficult position where they were besieged and starved at the Megiddo fortress for several months until they surrendered to Egypt. Although the King of Kadesh and some other leaders of the coalition escaped, primarily because the Egyptian soldiers had allowed themselves to be distracted by their looting spree, Thutmose III established himself as a fearless and victorious warrior who should not be challenged or disobeyed. He would later conquer the Kadesh and other states that had remained stubborn after their defeat in the Battle of Megiddo. The Battle of Megiddo also opened to the victorious warrior king an economic route that Kadesh had exercised control over as a crucial trade route to the Middle East and Asia when it rebelled against Egyptian rule. The spoils of war that went to the pharaoh and his soldiers were plentiful, but more importantly, all the conquered territories became vassals and sent tributes to Egypt, from the larger part of the Mediterranean region to other parts of the world where the pharaoh's forces and fame reached.

When Thutmose III defeated the King of Kadesh and his entire coalition, other states and kingdoms from far and wide were quick to make moves to be on the good side of the pharaoh, bringing large gifts and swearing allegiance to the warrior king. His victory also won him the great respect of other powers such as the Hittites, the powerful state that the rebelling kingdoms had recklessly decided to pay their tributes to before the Battle of Megiddo. There were about 20 other campaigns to keep his vassals in check in the Mediterranean region, as well as clashes between Egypt and big powers such as the Mitanni who, according to some scholars, were seriously defeated by Thutmose III on at least two different occasions. After every victory, Thutmose III and his forces would hold special ceremonies and make victory offerings to the gods. Their return to Egypt was always a great affair as they usually returned with human, agricultural, and mineral resources from the conquered states. All over his conquered territories, the pharaoh set up garrisons and enforced a strong military policy that protected his vassals. Although his tributes usually came as large items of economic value, there were also times when he received women as his tributes. This was the case when three Syrian sisters, Menhet, Menwi, and Merti were sent to the warrior king as tributes and joined the list of the king's lesser wives. During his reign, he built a royal retreat and relaxation place in Gurob, Faiyum, where he likely spent more time with his lesser wives and concubines. Also, it was probably one of his lesser wives who gave birth to Henuten, a royal woman believed to have been one of the daughters of Thutmose III.

Thutmose III married Queen Merytre-Hatshepsut, who gave birth to Princess Iset (apparently named after the mother of Thutmose III), two daughters named Meritamun C and Meritamun D, as well as Amenhotep II, the successor to the throne of Egypt after Thutmose III. Before he married Queen Merytre-Hatshepsut, he was married to Satiah (meaning "Daughter of the Moon"), who was not of royal birth and was the daughter of a royal nurse and possibly the mother of Prince Amenemhat. Below the rank of the Great Royal Wife was the Great Wife of the King, which was the position that Nebtu occupied. Also, it is possible that Thutmose III had married Hatshepsut's daughter and his half-sister, Neferure, and had a son with her before her early death.

At Armant, it is believed that Thutmose III renovated a temple built by Hatshepsut, which puts the relationship between the warrior king and his stepmother in a different light. Also, the fact that he built a temple with his stepmother in Medinet Habu in Thebes has encouraged many scholars to argue that their relationship must have been misunderstood over the years. Scholars have argued that it took at least a decade after Thutmose III began to rule Egypt before the monuments and traces of Hatshepsut's reign were hammered to ruin and wiped out of Egyptian history. They believe it is highly likely that those destroyed monuments had nothing to do with any animosity between Thutmose III and his stepmother. At El-Gabal el-Ahmar, meaning "the Red Hill," a very important site where quartzite was quarried and used for monuments under several ancient Egyptian kings, Thutmose III extracted quartzite to renovate the city complex at Heliopolis. He also extracted beautiful rocks and stones that he used to build a shrine at Heliopolis where he sometimes made offerings. From time to time, he held obelisk festivals and special offerings to celebrate the gods on behalf of whom the obelisks were erected. To honor the god of harvest and fertility, Min, he built a chapel in Panopolis in Upper Egypt. At Karnak, he expanded the temple of Amun and added a celebration hall to the temple. In addition, he built a massive temple and fortress in the northern region of Nubia known as Kalabsha. He also built a temple in honor of the Nubian god Dedun. The Temple of Kalabsha would later be expanded by Amenhotep II and Emperor Augustus in the Greco-Roman period.

At Abydos, Thutmose III built a temple in honor of Osiris and added massive statues of himself in the form of Osiris to the building. In the "Book of the Hidden Chamber," also known as Amduat (meaning "that which is in the netherworld"), which was found as a funerary text on the walls of the tomb of Thutmose III, the rejuvenation of Ra is described in a way that shows the sophistication of Egyptian literature. According to the text, which properly became part of Egyptian culture in the fifteenth century B.C.E., it is believed that the sun god considers the 12 hours of the day as rejuvenation and the 12 hours of the night as death. Subsequently, the inscription became an inspiration for the Egyptian "Book of the Dead." More than anything else, the Amduat talks about the unfriendly circumstances that the living should get familiar with before they die. It describes the challenging pathways, secret pathways, crisis pathways, secured pathways, the demons and evil spirits, and the scary people that the dead will encounter in their journey to the afterlife. In an explanation of the registers that make up the Amduat, it is said that:

> The first hour of the Amduat, divided in three main registers, presents various important and typical beings of the netherworld. The clear symmetrical structure, in particular in the upper and lower registers, with groups of nine gods alternating with groups of twelve goddesses, can be read as a symbolic representation of order which is always to be maintained in the mind of ancient Egyptians. The forces of chaos and evil, in fact, represented by the snake-shaped

Apophis, the most terrifying demon of the netherworld, is the main enemy which Ra encounters during his journey.

One of the key elements of the first hour of the Amduat are the solar baboons, represented in their typical crouching position, awaiting the arrival of Ra. Baboons are traditional members of the entourage of the sun god, accompanying him with music and dance. Their role here is to open the gates of the netherworld which are not actually depicted in the text.

The middle register is subdivided into two registers with the god Ra appearing as ram-headed in the upper one. He is shown within a shrine at the centre of his solar barque (known to Egyptians as Mesektet during the 12 hours of night), accompanied by various gods and, in front of him, is the adoring deceased, Nesmin. The register also contains two representations of Maat (the personified order of the world) and other deities as well as four human-headed stelae.

The lower middle register represents somehow a duplication of the previous register but this time Ra is represented in his solar bark as a scarab beetle, or Khepri, adored by two kneeling figures of Osiris. Having both the nocturnal (ram-headed) and rejuvenated morning (scarab beetle) forms of the sun-god makes absolutely clear, since the first hour of the night, the central message of the whole text: the concept of regeneration. This is indeed the final objective of the sun god's nocturnal path through the netherworld, which ends with his rebirth in the morning. (Royal Collection Trust, n.d.)

As a pharaoh who fought many battles and went on many military campaigns, Thutmose III surrounded himself with several courageous warriors and military heads, including Dedu, a security expert, leader of the Medjay troops, and royal envoy in Nubia where Thutmose III built a temple for their chief god, Dedun. Also, there was Benimeryt, the architect of the royal family and the supervisor of all the public projects of Thutmose III; Intef, a military governor and right-hand man of Thutmose III during many military expeditions; Thaneni, the Royal Scribe of Thutmose III and art director who was put in charge of the annals of Thutmose III at Karnak; and Djehuti, a valorous and brilliant military captain who fought exceptionally against the enemies of Egypt, achieved victories for Thutmose III, and won a golden collar from the pharaoh. According to the records, it was Djehuti who captured the city of Jaffa, an ancient port city in Southern Tel-Aviv-Yafo, using a cunning plan that would become very popular among military strategists many centuries later. Djehuti had faked his own defection from the camp of Thutmose III and Egypt to join the enemy coalition of which Jaffa was a notable part. Djehuti had gone to the gates of the port city with Egyptian soldiers, some of whom were disguised as his family members while the others were disguised as his private property in dozens of woven baskets. He promised to deliver Egypt, as well as specific items of interest, including the spoils of war, to the Jaffa coalition. Djehuti and his train of disguised soldiers were happily welcomed to the critical city, and they did well to capture it in no time, delivering a highly strategic location to Thutmose III who was well pleased with Djehuti and rewarded him bountifully. Among the many others who served Thutmose III, there was Roy, a military leader and the chief treasurer during the reign of the warrior king; Amun-Wosret, the vizier during his reign who contributed massively to his war efforts; Min, a judge, a respected leader of priests, a military expert, and the private tutor and military trainer of Prince Amenhotep II; Nenwif, a high-ranking military leader and commander of the Egyptian cavalrymen; Amenemhab, who achieved several heroic feats on and off the battlefield while Thutmose III was in power; and Menkheperresenb, an Amun prophet, architect, and overseer of the "Gold and Silver Houses," the royal residence of Thutmose III at Thebes.

Another important official in the court of the warrior king was a War Scribe known as Thunany. Thunany followed Thutmose III on his many military expeditions and recorded what he saw and heard at different points in those campaigns. His tomb at Thebes has been a great go-to place for visual details of the campaigns of Thutmose III. Both Userman and Rekhmire served Thutmose III as his viziers, and Rekhmire also served as the ears and scribe of the king sometimes. On the tomb of Rekhmire, the Eighteenth Dynasty vizier who served Thutmose III and his successor, information about the position of the vizier and his functions is presented in impressive detail. Thutmose III had given Rekhmire the imperial approval to make sure that the state was well-run and that the vizier's office, which is probably similar to the office of a prime minister in the modern world, promotes the policies and wishes of the pharaoh for his empire. Thutmose III put Rekhmire in charge of tax and legal administration, conflict resolution, labor and agriculture, as well as many other duties pertaining to the day-to-day running of the state and the promotion of the pharaoh's policies. The reign of Thutmose III pushed ancient Egypt to become the first in many areas, particularly as the leading empire in the world at the time from politics to culture, literature, and economy. Before the Thirteenth Dynasty when Egypt began to make its own coins, different forms of payments and barter systems existed in Egypt, and during the reign of Thutmose III metal tokens measured by weight were exchanged for goods and services. Apart from introducing this form of monetary system during his reign, he also brought wood and minerals from Cyprus and other conquered territories to ancient Egypt to boost the economy. To facilitate the ease of movement, particularly for commercial and military activities, Thutmose III reopened the canals close to Dal Island along the Great Cataract and enhanced access to parts of Nubia that were strategically important to the goal of Egypt. Records would later show that he brought Upper and Lower Kush (Nubia) under Egyptian control, and they paid tributes to Egypt.

Thirteen years before his death at 83 years old, he went on his last military expedition and brought more territories under Egyptian control, receiving a lot more tributes as a result. Before the end of his reign, Thutmose III had become the greatest conqueror of Egypt with more than 350 cities brought under his control. He expanded the boundaries of the empire in every way possible and took Egypt to the greatest heights imaginable for a big power in the New Kingdom. Thutmose III died before his Great Royal Wife, Queen Merytre-Hatshepsut, who was alive until her son Amenhotep II was well into his reign.

Chapter 10:

Akhenaten (1353 B.C.E.–1336

B.C.E.)

Also known as Neferkheperure-Waenre (meaning "The Unique Transformation of Re") or Amenhotep IV, Akhenaten was a bold king who introduced to Egypt a set of radical religious and artistic reforms that set him apart from all the rulers of Egypt before him. As a prince, he was known as Prince Amenhotep and sometime around the last part of his father's reign, he became a co-regent. Born to Queen Tiye and Pharaoh Amenhotep III, Prince Amenhotep was raised as the junior brother to Prince Thutmose, the crown prince before him. He also had Iset, Beketaten, and Sitamun, among others, as his sisters. After 30 years on the throne of Egypt, Amenhotep III celebrated the Heb-Sed festival, which was usually celebrated in ancient Egypt after the 30th regnal year of a pharaoh and every 3 years after that. Prince Thutmose is believed to have been absent from that festival, which is why scholars agree that he must have died before the festival.

The one who became crown prince after Prince Thutmose's early death, Prince Amenhotep, married Nefertiti while he was still a co-regent to his father, and they became parents to six girls that included Meketaten, Meritaten, and Setepenre. Meketaten died in childbirth and Smenkhare, the husband to one of Akhenaten's daughters, Meritaten, probably became a co-regent to Akhenaten, especially because he ascended to the throne after the death of Akhenaten who did not have a male child with Nefertiti. Nefertiti is believed to have suddenly disappeared from royal portraits and stories after a while in Amarna. Akhenaten also married another woman named Kiya with whom he had one daughter and two sons. When he became the king of Egypt, he was known as Amenhotep IV, although this name would change early in his reign to Akhenaten, in honor of the god he promoted above all the other gods (including Amun) that the Egyptians had always known: Aten. Later, he would claim to have been shown a vision by Aten, the sun disk deity, which led him to an unknown site that would later be known as Akhetaten.

Akhenaten had the site developed into a beautiful city with different impressive structures befitting a new religious and administrative capital. He also introduced building stones known as *talatat* because of their nice and small block shapes that made them easier to make and move around. This helped to accelerate the building of the structures that beautified Akhetaten—from the temple of Aten to the royal palace—and turned it into the beautiful city that was known as the Horizon of Aten. The city built by Akhenaten is known as Amarna today. Akhenaten's mother Queen Tiye, who survived her husband Amenhotep III, would later move to Akhetaten to live with her son before she passed on to the afterlife.

When Akhenaten made Aten the chief god of Egypt and moved to the new capital city, he made a lot of enemies in religion, politics, the military, and society in general, particularly the ordinary people of ancient Egypt who were confused and angry by the strange behavior and policies of their king. To reduce the power of the High Priests of Amun, he dismissed them and proscribed their Amun. Subsequently, he made himself the only priest of Aten (although he would appoint Meryre, an official that was very close to him, in the final leg of his reign as the High Priest of Aten) and later made himself a god too. As the only High Priest of Aten, Akhenaten personally wrote a wonderful piece of worship poetry that he called "Hymn to the Aten" and used it to encourage the people to come through him to reach Aten. In his high praises of Aten, he wrote: "Thou arisest fair in the horizon of Heaven, O Living Aten, Beginner of Life… there is none who knows thee save thy son Akhenaten. Thou hast made him wise in thy plans and thy power" (Clayton, 1994).

In addition, Akhenaten led the offerings and ceremonies held for Aten at Amarna and worshiped the solar disk deity until the end of his reign in the New Kingdom. In politics, he retired or removed many of the old court officials and replaced them with new officials, although the policy has been criticized by some scholars because it is believed that the inexperience of the new officials did not help Egypt. According to the analyses of some scholars, these changes made by Akhenaten happened too quickly for the majority of ancient Egyptians, and it was extremely hard to make sense of any reason why they would abandon Amun, Horus, Osiris, and all the deities they had always known for one god of the solar disk that they barely knew. In this regard, one argument has encouraged us to see Akhenaten "as a remarkable and somewhat tragic figure because he seems to have perceived the irrelevance of much of the thought of his day" (Kemp, 2018). However, another argument tells us that the reaction of ancient Egyptians to Akhenaten's reforms was a sign of what human beings were in the past and what they are now in the modern world. This situation has been explained further in this manner (Kemp, 2018):

> Although Akhenaten's twin visions of a monarchy worshipped for itself, and of a rationale that was so simple and direct as to release the king from the shrouds of mystery, failed to convince his contemporaries and died with him, it offered a glimpse of a future that is still with us. Akhenaten's kingship provides an unintended caricature of all modern leaders who indulge in the trappings of charismatic display. The Egyptians themselves did not like what they saw. It evidently offended their sense of good taste. After his death, they returned to intellectual compromise and wrapped again the nakedness of monarchy in the shrouds of transcendental imaginings. (p. 275)

Meanwhile, at Amarna, Akhenaten and Nefertiti produced Ankhesenamen, the lady who would later marry King Tut. At the same time, Akhenaten caused a lot of radical changes to happen in Egyptian art during his reign in the New Kingdom. The same energy he used to push Aten forward as the leading deity in Egypt was used to tilt the artistic creations of his time in a new direction. In the artistic work showing the royal family, the new form of art, which is known as Amarna art, was very different from what was previously known before Akhenaten. The big changes made to the shape and size of the head, the changes made to the size of the lips and some other parts of the body like the stomach and bottom, so that they became enlarged, were seriously far apart from what was the previous way of depicting the royal family. The realistic way that the Amarna art depicted the royal family has earned Akhenaten heaps of praise and positive commentaries among scholars. In one of the portraits discovered by archeologists, a scene is portrayed of how affectionate Akhenaten was with Queen Nefertiti and their children. The portrait shows Akhenaten and Nefertiti sharing a bonding moment with three of their daughters.

During Akhenaten's reign, the Egyptian empire continued to have a strong hold on its vassals and a great relationship with its allies, but as time went on, the pharaoh's radical policies began to fuel an increase in discontent in ancient Egypt and create chaos in the vassal states and conquered territories. Records of the correspondence between Akhenaten and the rulers of Egypt's vassal states known as the Amarna Letters have shown that the leaders of some vassal states occasionally wrote to Akhenaten to clear their names when issues came up that could cause the full anger of the Egyptian empire to be brought down upon them. An example of this is the letter written to Akhenaten by a Jerusalem prince known as Abdu Heba. Abdu Heba's message to Akhenaten was to clear his name and assure the pharaoh that what a Hebron prince known as Shuwardata had reported about him was not true. The prince of Hebron had written to Akhenaten alleging that Abdu Heba was attacking cities that were part of the Egyptian empire with a tribe of nomads known as the Apiru.

In another letter, Abdu Heba appealed to Akhenaten to caution the occupying troops from Egypt that were making his life uncomfortable by stealing from his palace while drinking recklessly and threatening his life at the same time. In a different appeal to Akhenaten, the Prince of Megiddo at the time, known as Biridiya, wrote to Akhenaten to request the redeployment of Egyptian troops that had been previously withdrawn from Megiddo by Akhenaten. Biridiya believed the withdrawal of the troops had caused Megiddo to be in a bad situation in which they were besieged by enemy troops. In the Near East, the Kassite king known as Kurigalzu capitalized on the weakening power of Egypt under Akhenaten and attacked and seized the capital of one of the vassal city-states of Egypt known as Susa. For some vassal states like Gezer where the prince had an issue involving land with other small territories, Akhenaten sent some Egyptian soldiers to put the issue to bed, but the same cannot be said for the Ruler of Byblos (modern-day Lebanon), where invading Amurru forces, led by their king, sacked the kingdom and exiled their king in spite of their appeals to Akhenaten to deploy Egyptian troops to save them. It is possible that the chaos in Egypt had worsened at this time and Akhenaten was unable to send troops to vassal states when needed. The same thing that happened in Byblos happened to the people of Accho (in modern-day Israel) where the prince of the city-state, Zatatna, wrote to Akhenaten appealing for the support of Egypt to defeat the enemy forces threatening their freedom and territory. They did not get any troops from Egypt.

Although some scholars have argued that Akhenaten did not show any interest in military campaigns during his reign, there are suggestions in the scenes and letters found at Amarna that there might in fact have been some campaigns during his reign, particularly in the Mediterranean region. According to some scenes discovered at Hermopolis (a city between Lower and Upper Egypt), an amazing depiction of Nefertiti, Akhenaten's Great Royal Wife, was found on some talatat blocks showing her crushing the enemies of Egypt. There are no records showing that Nefertiti went on any military campaign, but the art can be interpreted as one of the strengths of Amarna art, which showed women as beautiful and powerful enough to defend Egypt with their physical strength. Also, it is possible that the artistic work was meant to portray the level of Nefertiti's involvement in the imperial government of Akhenaten who, at some point in his reign, showed less and less interest in politics, diplomacy, and administration and mostly focused on worshiping Aten. At the same time, there is really no strong evidence that Akhenaten led any military campaign himself, especially since the vassal states of Egypt were either occupied by Egyptian forces or mercenaries working for Egypt.

Among the many officials who served Akhenaten was Mai, a military leader who also served Akhenaten as the chief supervisor of the Royal Palace at Amarna; Shuta, also a military commander who served Akhenaten mostly in vassal states and faced several rebellions because of the chaos in Egypt during the final days of the reign of Akhenaten; Ramose, the vizier who served Akhenaten for a short time before he gave up the ghost and could not move to Amarna with the pharaoh; Parennefer, Akhenaten's private butler who served him throughout his life; Tutu, who was the chief official in charge of the Royal Household; Mahu, a powerful police official who commanded the Egyptian police at Amarna; Yuti, an artist who was also the official sculptor of the royal family and did many artistic works at Amarna; and Pentu, the royal physician who served Akhenaten throughout his reign at Amarna.

There was also Yanhamu, an Egyptian who served Akhenaten in the position of governor of conquered Palestine and also kept tabs on the neighboring vassal states of Egypt. When things began to go bad under Akhenaten, he wrote letters describing the situation to the pharaoh.

It is believed that Akhenaten was not a very outgoing king and that he lived a solitary life. The cause of Akhenaten's death is unknown, and the whereabouts of his remains have been the subject of endless debates among scholars and Egyptologists.

Chapter 11:

Xerxes (486 B.C.E.–465 B.C.E.)

In the Late Period (664 B.C.E.–332 B.C.E.), the Persians, a nomadic Indo-European people, had started to grow in power and fame, and their imperial expansion goal had kicked off with promising results. After invading and conquering Egypt, a man named Cambyses kicked off the Twenty-Seventh Dynasty as the first Persian to rule Egypt ca. 525 B.C.E., making Egypt a province of Persia. He was succeeded by Darius I before Xerxes I, the son of Darius I and Queen Atossa, became the next ruler of Egypt of Persian origin. However, Xerxes I was not the same ruler as Cambyses or Darius I as far as respecting the traditional ways of ancient Egyptians was concerned. Cambyses took on the Egyptian throne name Mesutire, meaning "Offspring of Re." Darius I, on his own part, took on the throne name Seture, meaning "Likeness of Re." However, when it came to Xerxes, he disrespected the gods of ancient Egyptians, rejected any Egyptian title or throne name, imposed the culture of the Persians on the Egyptians, and mercilessly put down any revolt by the Egyptians before it had barely started.

Egypt was required to pay tributes to the Persian Empire and regular taxes were imposed on the people to help Persia fund its numerous military campaigns. According to an account of the reign of the Persians in Egypt found on the temple-like tomb of Petosiris, the High Priest of Thoth at Hermopolis Magna, "[a]ll the temples were without their servants and the priests fled, not knowing what was happening" (Snape, 2021). The Persian army was probably at one of its strongest under Xerxes I, with some suggestions claiming that the army may have reached up to one or two million in size at its zenith. There are scholars who believe it is likely that the reason why Xerxes became a heavy-handed ruler in Egypt was due to some of the circumstances he met when he ascended to the throne. Before the death of Darius I, there had been a rebellion in the Nile Delta that Xerxes I had to deal with when he became the king. His lesson from dealing with that rebellion, it is said, may have been to change the style of Persian rule in Egypt to a heavy-handed style.

When there was a revolt against Persian rule in Babylonia, Xerxes mobilized the Persian army, which included many conscripted Egyptians, and re-established his power over the Babylonians. To teach the Babylonians a lesson they would not forget easily, Xerxes commanded his soldiers to loot their resources and properties and to also destroy their temples, particularly the temple of Marduk, the Babylonian god of Heaven and Earth, their principal god. Because of the way Xerxes disrespected their god and treated them with disdain and a lack of compassion, the Babylonians revolted at least two more times during the reign of Xerxes. The Achaemenid ruler eventually decided to besiege Babylonia to substantially reduce the possibility of another revolt or Babylonia becoming a huge threat in the future. For Xerxes, Babylonia was an important part of the empire, particularly because the Achaemenid Empire really began with Cyrus the Great conquering Babylonia in addition to the Median Empire.

Xerxes I was married to Amestris, a Persian woman with whom he had Artaxerxes I, his heir and successor to the throne of Egypt. Like Darius I, Xerxes made attempts to conquer more territories and expand the boundaries of the Persian Empire, but when he tried to do that with the Greeks, the goal became more difficult to achieve. It is believed that Xerxes I recorded some victories against the Greeks, particularly after he captured the great city-state of ancient Greece: Athens. This victory was a great boost of morale for the Persian army that had suffered a defeat under Darius I in 490 B.C.E. at Marathon, ten years before Athens fell to the forces of Xerxes, and what was left of the city was laid to ruin; however, when the Greeks reorganized themselves and confronted the army of Xerxes that was already high on its early victories—with Xerxes himself mounting a very high throne from which he could watch the clash—they got to defeat the Persians and reclaim their lost city. Many soldiers died during the sea and land battles against the Greeks, and the defeat affected the morale of Xerxes I and the Persian army. Ariabignes, a brother of Xerxes I leading one of the Persian vessels fighting against the Greeks, was killed during the battle.

In spite of his disrespect for Egyptian gods and tradition, Xerxes made sure that he maintained the administrative system that was operated by the Egyptians before they were conquered. Like Darius and Cambyses before him, the decision to continue that one thing, after destroying or disrespecting everything else, was to ensure the ease of governing Egypt as a province of the Persian Empire, with a principal Persian leader known as the satrap leading the conquered province. It is believed that the satraps were usually descendants of nobles and people from the upper class in Persian society. However, the satraps did not have the king's blind approval to act without accountability in the territories they were charged with. At least once every year, the elite private or secret army of Persian kings, known as "the Eyes and Ears of the King," would conduct an official inspection of Persian provinces such as Egypt. Some scholars have argued that Xerxes I never stepped foot in Egypt, although some accounts also argue that he was in Egypt only a couple of times.

Among those who served Xerxes I was his brother, a prince named Achaemenes who was made satrap in Egypt. As the eyes and ears of Xerxes I in Egypt, Achaemenes went above and beyond to satisfy his brother. At the well-known battle against the Greeks, the famous second invasion of Greece known as the Battle of Salamis, Achaemenes forcefully brought many Egyptians to war and when the Persians were disgraced and lost, he became much crueler toward the Egyptians. He was killed on the battlefield when he tried to suppress a rebellion in Egypt. Apart from Achaemenes, there was also a famous and feared military general called Megabyzus who served Xerxes I. It is believed that Xerxes I was assassinated by a man named Artabanus, the commander of the palace guard. Artabanus also killed Darius, a son and crown prince of Xerxes I, before he was slain in hand-to-hand combat by Artaxerxes I, the son of Xerxes I and the successor to the throne of Egypt. Artabanus was part of the conspiracy that led to the assassination of Xerxes after 21 years on the throne.

Chapter 12:

The Fear and the Power of the

Pharaohs

There is really no doubt that the ancient Egyptian culture that Egyptologists and the rest of the world celebrate and shed light on in the modern era had the Egyptian pharaohs at its center. The role of the pharaohs in the progress of ancient Egypt's cultural, social, and political life was approved by the people as divine and extremely important. When the Egyptians bestowed the highest symbol of unity, progress, and divine perfection on the pharaoh after the Unification of Upper and Lower Egypt, there was no telling what would come of that great first step, but many of the most memorable things we know of ancient Egypt today are the things we know about the pharaohs who ruled the great civilization at one point or the other. The pharaohs were more than just rulers; their rise and fall were the rise and fall of the whole of Egypt. When the pharaohs fell, dynasties and centuries of progress fell with them; when they got back on their feet, dynasties and breathtaking innovations rose with them.

At different points in the history of ancient Egypt, the pharaohs were at the forefront of defending, promoting, establishing, and solidifying the ways of the Egyptians and the uniqueness of their civilization, which quickly became the ways of many other parts of the world. Before the Romans conquered Egypt, the outsiders who ruled Egypt— from the Hyksos to Persians, Alexander the Great, and the Ptolemies—met a system they could not help but work with because it would have been silly to try to destroy a system that had gone through many corrections for many centuries. As rigid as the Romans were, there were aspects of Egyptian culture and civilization they could not ignore, things that the Romans were eager to promote and practice. From Narmer to Cleopatra VII, the progress, challenges, and victories recorded by ancient Egyptians throughout the course of their civilization explain why it is important to understand the true uniqueness and relationship of ancient Egypt with the state of things in the world now. The many gods that the Egyptians worshiped and the ones they classified into different ranks and gave different meanings became the media by which the complicated nature of our world was viewed and interpreted. Those interpretations, symbols, and media of connecting the physical world to the supernatural world have inspired devotions of many kinds that have lasted into our time. There are artistic, political, cultural, religious, and other sides of life that we can now trace back to Egyptian civilization and the innovations and lessons it produced.

The rare radical reforms of Akhenaten in the New Kingdom have been repeated in different parts of the world, whether in Europe, America, or some other place, and they have inspired several great ideas under the umbrella of freedom of thought. From being a divided people with different cultural and political goals, the ancient Egyptians taught the world how much can be achieved in a united nation and what victories can be expected when efforts go into building great cultural, religious, and political structures. The way the reign of every pharaoh was connected with the reigns of the previous and future pharaohs created a pattern of systemic marriage that served the purpose of promoting cultural, artistic, political, and societal confidence, cooperation, and innovation. Milestones like the most advanced pyramids and the most developed army of the time were achieved after the pharaohs who were predecessors laid down a certain formula for their successors to use and improve. At the center of their ways of life was the *maat* philosophy, which helped to put things in perspective as far as achieving order, unity, and progress in any and every aspect of life was concerned.

After agreeing that order was important, the ancient Egyptians designed their society so that there was one. At the top of the social ladder was the most important family in their world, the royal family, with the pharaoh being the number one royal that mattered since the pharaoh was both a human and divine figure. The royal family was joined by nobles, priests, physicians, and military commanders in the same class. This class shared and controlled political power in ancient Egypt. They decided how the policies, laws, and wishes of the pharaohs were followed and executed. The upper class was followed by another group in which sculptors, painters, and other artists, as well as artisans, were to be found. The next group consisted of the farmers who worked very hard to keep the people well-fed and the economy in good shape. The farmers paid taxes in grains to officials appointed by the pharaoh or the vizier, and the grains were used to feed government officials and stored for the harsh days of drought and famine.

Although the farmers belonged to the lower class, they had a position higher than the slaves and servants who were made to do menial work in ancient Egyptian society. This social structure was not achieved in one day, but it helped to create an understanding that placed people at different levels and made their roles in society really clear. The nice thing about the structure was that it allowed people to move from a lower level to a higher one once they had achieved the necessary conditions that would make them qualified for it. For some people who were from a lower class, they achieved a change in social status by marrying into a higher class. It was the same for members of a foreign state or tribe who wanted to become Egyptians; they married into an Egyptian family and socially progressed over the years by joining the military, the order of the priests, or becoming court officials. Egyptian society also had some customs in relation to the relationship between parents and their children. It has already been noted that most Egyptian sons learnt the same trade as their father, whether he was a peasant farmer or a king. Equally, girls were expected to follow in their mothers' footsteps and grow up to take on domestic tasks" (Snape, 2021). When it came to the social differences in the roles of men and women in ancient Egypt, multiple sources have shown that there was not much. According to Khalil et al. (2017):

> Unlike other ancient societies, women in Ancient Egypt had a high degree of equal opportunity and freedom...Ancient Egyptians (women and men) were firmly equal. Interestingly, ancient sources indicate that women were qualified to sue and obtain contracts incorporating any lawful settlements, such as marriage, separation, property, and jobs.

Writing on the same phenomenon in ancient Egypt that was apparently strange to him, the Greek historian Herodotus said (Tyldesley, 1995):

[T]he Egyptian themselves, in most of their manners and customs, exactly reverse the common practices of mankind. For example, the women attend the markets and trade, while the men sit at home and weave at the loom. The women likewise carry burdens upon their shoulders while the men carry them upon their heads. Sons need not support their parents unless they chose, but daughters must, whether they chose to or not. (p. 20)

Meanwhile, because of the short life expectancy during that time, marriage was encouraged at a young age. In one of the surviving written pieces of evidence from ancient Egypt, a message for the young men said, "take to yourselves a wife while you are young, so that she may give you a son. You should begat him for yourself when you are still young, and should live to see him become a man" (Tyldesley, 1995). At the same time, the people praised the gods for blessing them with the Nile, which became the source of natural fertilizer for their agricultural endeavors. From grains to fruits, vegetables, herbs, and industrial crops, the ancient Egyptians spent much of their time growing the crops that were crucial to their survival and advancement and used them for food, commerce, medicine, and many types of important articles. In spite of the circumstances in which they lived, which were very different from the advantages that make the modern world different from theirs, the Egyptians were creative in their approach to large-scale farming and gardening, and they used different methods to achieve the best possible results "including the use of irrigation systems, cloning, propagation and training" (Food and Agriculture Organization of the United Nations, 2020).

In addition to their domestic innovative methods in agriculture, they also expanded their access to the vast international markets that existed in the near and far city-states. The pharaohs set up departments for different sectors and appointed capable hands as court officials to increase Egypt's chances of securing the agricultural products they lacked. Some of these agricultural products, in addition to natural and mineral resources, were secured from other states through trade and barter of different mineral resources. There is recorded evidence of these dealings and exchanges between Egypt and Nubia, Punt, Libya, Greece, and other regions. In territories that were invaded and conquered by the Egyptian army, these resources were basically looted or taken to Egypt as spoils of war. There is a lot that the ancient Egyptians achieved with agriculture, and according to the Food and Agriculture Organization of the United Nations (2020):

> Over 2,000 different species of flowering or aromatic plants have been found in tombs. Papyrus was an extremely versatile crop that grew wild and was also cultivated. The roots of the plant were eaten as food, but it was primarily used as an industrial crop. The stem of the plant was used to make boats, mats, and paper. Flax was another important industrial crop that had several uses. Its primary use was in the production of rope, and for linen which was the Egyptians' principal material for making their clothing. Henna was grown for the production of dye.

In spite of the kindness of the Nile, there were periods when ancient Egyptians had to deal with drought and famine, such as the famine experienced by ancient Egyptians during the reign of Djoser or the climate change that turned fertile land into desert, but the way the Egyptians dealt with these extreme environmental challenges—from developing storage systems to improving communication and cooperation strategies—showed how capable they were of staying resilient and finding solutions. According to Nguyen (2021), the resilience of ancient Egyptians is something that we can learn from in the modern world:

> Climate stress, including the decline in Nile flooding, caused significant misery for the ancient Egyptians. But the ways that the society managed to stay afloat and cope with the effects of uncontrollable environmental change offer important lessons...Ancient societies were extremely resilient...They would find solutions to get by, to survive. Migration was the most extreme one. There was also increased localized governance in response to the effects of climate change.

Apart from agriculture and dealing with environmental challenges, ancient Egypt developed greatly in artistic innovations over many centuries and inspired admiration and imitation among its contemporaries. From the Stepped Pyramid of Djoser to the Great Pyramid at Giza, the scarabs, wall paintings, reliefs, Amarna art, and much more, ancient Egyptians did not shy away from the dedication and commitment required for great things to be done. The art produced in ancient Egypt showed the different sides of Egypt, from social classes to religion and politics. Important actors in Egyptian politics such as the viziers or the High Priests who led festivals and offerings, were also shown in reliefs, sculptures, and scenes of what happened during that time. To its contemporaries, ancient Egypt was a place where miracles happened. According to one account, there is inadequate knowledge and appreciation (outside the circle of Egyptologists, classicists, and scholars) for the people and cultures that were inspired by the artistic abilities of ancient Egyptians (Smee, 2018):

> What stimulated the Greek sculptural revolution, recognized to this day as among the crowning glories of Western civilization? In a word, Egypt. Without the phenomenon of Greek artists traveling to Egypt, returning home and trying to emulate the scale, skill and ambition of what they had seen, ancient Greek sculpture is impossible to imagine.

The Egyptian military also went through a series of phases and changes in strength and objective over the different dynastic periods. The Predynastic Period was a period of conflict between Upper and Lower Egypt, and the people saw more militias and tribal warfare than an organized state military. The challenge of building a state where the people of the Nile Valley and the Nile Delta were united continued through the Early Dynastic Period and the early pharaohs were focused on making sure the state had clear boundaries and was protected from invaders and hostile enemies. They were also focused on completely ending the division and fighting within Egyptian territory, protecting the people, and solidifying the strengths of the state. Little by little, they achieved this and the power of the pharaoh became clearer and stronger, both physically and spiritually. By the Old Kingdom, the pharaohs had consolidated the Unification of the Two Lands, and the focus of the state was, to an increasing extent, shifting toward foreign territories. At the same time, the fame and power of the pharaohs were no longer in question, and the military had become a true symbol of how powerful the state had become. Egyptian troops were growing in numbers both on land and water, and their campaigns during the reigns of the different pharaohs had become a sure way of demonstrating the power of Egypt to their neighbors across the Near East and the Mediterranean (Bunson, 2002).

Those military campaigns, although fought with basic weapons such as bows and arrows and a limited number of shields, were also used to secure food and all kinds of resources for the Egyptian people (Bunson, 2002). In this regard, the pharaohs were seen as defenders and providers by the people. They were feared for the power they displayed with the military forces within and particularly outside ancient Egypt, crushing their enemies left, right, and center, and they were also feared as divine beings who had the power to shape the present and impact the journey of the dead in the afterlife. The pharaohs were physical images of the gods, and the gods were somehow the pharaohs. Apart from the military campaigns of the pharaohs in the Old Kingdom, another practice was becoming more popular, and the pharaohs, as well as the priests, were at the forefront of promoting it. This was the growing cult of Osiris and the promotion of the role of Osiris in the journey of the dead to the afterlife. Records have shown how the funerary ceremonies for the dead included appearing in the Judgment Hall of Osiris where Osiris and 42 judges placed the heart of the dead on a scale of good and evil and decided whether the dead deserved to be happy or suffer in the afterlife, mostly after the confessions of the soul of the dead. Although the poor and those generally in the lower class of Egyptian society were not able to do these confessions because they had to be written by the scribes, they had their own way of appealing to Osiris and his judges to grant them a happy experience in the afterlife (Bunson, 2002).

According to one of the three parts in the "Chapter of the Judgement of Osiris," in the Egyptian "Book of the Dead," each dead person had confessions that they needed to recite to Osiris before their journey to the afterlife. These texts and confessions are signs that under the watch of the pharaohs, ancient Egypt developed many forms of its rich literature and philosophy and matched them with the aspirations of the Egyptian people. The first part of the "Chapter of the Judgement of Osiris" goes as follows (Budge & Wilson, 2016):

> Homage to thee, O Great God, Lord of Maati, I have come to thee, O my Lord, that I may behold thy beneficence. I know thee, and I know thy name, and the names of the Forty-Two

who live with thee in the Hall of Maati, who keep ward over sinners, and feed upon their blood on the day of estimating characters before Un-Nefer...Behold, I have come to thee, and I have brought maat (i.e., truth, integrity) to thee. I have destroyed sin for thee. I have not sinned against men. I have not oppressed [my] kinsfolk. I have done no wrong in the place of truth. I have not known worthless folk. I have not wrought evil. I have not defrauded the oppressed one of his goods. I have not done the things that the gods abominate. I have not vilified a servant to his master. I have not caused pain. I have not let any man hunger. I have made no one to weep. I have not committed murder. I have not commanded any to commit murder for me. I have inflicted pain on no man. I have not defrauded the temples of their oblations. I have not purloined the cakes of the gods. I have not stolen the offerings to the spirits (i.e., the dead). I have not committed fornication. I have not polluted myself in the holy places of the god of my city. I have not diminished from the bushel. I did not encroach on the fields [of others]. I have not added to the weights of the scales. I have not misread the pointer of the scales. I have not taken milk from the mouths of children. I have not driven cattle from their pastures. I have not snared the birds of the gods. I have not caught fish with fish of their kind. I have not stopped water [when it should flow]. I have not cut the dam of a canal. I have not altered the times of the chosen meat offerings. I have not turned away the cattle [intended for] offerings. I have not repulsed the god at his appurtenances. I am pure. I am pure. I am pure. (p. 26)

For a little more than 100 years after the end of the Old Kingdom, ancient Egypt was seized by the chaos of the First Intermediate Period, and the military was divided. The next Intermediate Period that followed the Middle Kingdom, known as the Second Intermediate Period, was also a period of chaos that was waiting for the Third Intermediate Period that followed the New Kingdom. In the Third Intermediate Period, the chaos and division in ancient Egypt went on for a little more than 400 years before the arrival of the Late Period and the Greco-Roman Period. For the whole of these interconnected periods, the Egyptian military went through different phases of change, import, and function. In the fullness of time, the history of the

Egyptian civilization and the journey of the pharaohs as the central figures of those periods were only richer for it.

Conclusion

Whenever a history as rich and intimidating as the ancient Egyptian civilization is on the table for discussion, whether in the pages of books or on any platform for spreading knowledge, one thing we can all agree on is the fact that the conversation never ends. There are too many sides to the history of ancient Egypt. The civilization produced so much glory, lessons, awe, and inspiration for both the ancient world and what the world has become now. There are more aspects of the Egyptian civilization that we do *not* know than we do know, in spite of centuries of information, research, and more information. There are pharaohs that we know only a little of their reign, but the little we know about these pharaohs has sparked much curiosity and appreciation in many of us. Also, there are pharaohs and important personalities whose contributions we may know, but their disappearance from the scenes of history has never been known to us.

It is possible that we may never know the end of the richness of ancient Egypt. The civilization has given us a whole lot that makes us think we do not even have enough. We keep wanting more and more information. At the same time, there are things that happened in those days, such as the role of women and the respect that women enjoyed in society, that make us wonder if and when we will be able to achieve that level of advanced social model in our time. The things that the human race has held on to from that era, the knowledge we gained and the lessons we learned in politics, religion, art, law, etc., are things that will continue to guide our decisions and innovations in the modern world. Although we may not be aware of many things as far as the ancient Egyptian civilization is concerned, we can at least appreciate the fact that we have some crucial information to make our own world richer and our appreciation of our world better.

References

Budge, E. A. W., & Wilson, E. (2016). *The ancient Egyptian Book of the Dead: Prayers, incantations, and other texts from the Book of the Dead.* (E. Wilson, Ed.). Quarto Publishing Group USA.

Bunson, M. (2002). *Encyclopedia of ancient Egypt.* Facts on File.

Calvert, A. (2022, February 4). *Predynastic and Early Dynastic, an introduction.* Smarthistory. https://smarthistory.org/predynastic-early-dynastic-introduction/

Clayton, P. A. (1994). *Chronicle of the Pharaohs: The reign-by-reign record of the rulers and dynasties of ancient Egypt.* Thames and Hudson.

Food and Agriculture Organization of the United Nations. (2020, December 6). *Ancient Egyptian agriculture.* FAO. https://www.fao.org/country-showcase/item-detail/en/c/1287824/

Garland, R. (2012). *The other side of history: Daily life in the ancient world.* The Teaching Company, LLC.

Hitchins, D. (n.d.). *Khufu's vision for Akhet Khufu?* Prof's Ancient Egypt. Retrieved January 15, 2023, from https://egypt.hitchins.net/the-pyramids/khufus-vision-for-akhet.html

Holmes, A. (2011). *Ancient Egypt: History in an hour.* HarperCollins Publishers.

Johnson, P. (2012). *The civilization of ancient Egypt.* HarperCollins.

Kemp, B. J. (2018). *Ancient Egypt: Anatomy of a civilization.* Taylor & Francis.

Khalil, R., Moustafa, A. A., Moftah, M. Z., & Karim, A. A. (2017, January 5). How knowledge of ancient Egyptian women can influence today's gender role: Does history matter in Gender Psychology? *Frontiers in Psychology, 07.* 10.3389/fpsyg.2016.02053

Livius. (2020, June 23). *Den.* Livius.org. https://www.livius.org/articles/person/den/

Lloyd, A. B. (Ed.). (2014). *A companion to ancient Egypt.* Wiley.

Marshall Cavendish Corporation. (2011). *Ancient Egypt and the Near East: An illustrated history.* Marshall Cavendish Reference.

Mertz, B. (2009). *Temples, tombs, and hieroglyphs: A popular history of ancient Egypt.* HarperCollins.

Nguyen, L. (2021, August 2). *Forever changes: Climate lessons from ancient Egypt.* YaleNews. https://news.yale.edu/2021/08/02/forever-changes-climate-lessons-ancient-egypt

Romer, J. (2013). *A history of ancient Egypt: From the first farmers to the Great Pyramid.* Penguin Books.

Royal Collection Trust. (n.d.). *Egypt - Section of the papyrus belonging to Nesmin, with the first hour of the Amduat.* Royal Collection Trust. Retrieved January 19, 2023, from https://www.rct.uk/collection/1145266/section-of-the-papyrus-belonging-to-nesmin-with-the-first-hour-of-the-amduat

Shaw, I. (Ed.). (2003). *The Oxford history of ancient Egypt.* OUP Oxford.

Smee, S. (2018, June 22). *From the Pharaohs to Cleopatra and Julius Caesar: How Egypt influenced Greece and Rome.* The Washington Post. https://www.washingtonpost.com/entertainment/museums/from-the-pharaohs-to-cleopatra-and-julius-caesar-how-egypt-influenced-greece-and-rome/2018/06/22/96c65b24-73e8-11e8-b4b7-308400242c2e_story.html

Snape, S. R. (2021). *Ancient Egypt: The definitive visual history.* Dorling Kindersley Limited.

Tyldesley, J. (1995). *Daughters of Isis: Women of ancient Egypt.* Penguin Books Limited.

Van Basten, T. D. (2016). *Ancient Egypt: Egyptology—the study of ancient Egyptian history.* CreateSpace Independent Publishing Platform.

Vorster, L. (2016, January 1). *The Badarian culture of ancient Egypt in context: Critical evaluation.* Academia. https://www.academia.edu/72581833/The_Badarian_culture_of_ancient_Egypt_in_context_critical_evaluation

Wilkinson, R. H. (2003). *The complete gods and goddesses of ancient Egypt.* Thames & Hudson.

Wilkinson, T. (2014). *The Nile: A journey downriver through Egypt's past and present.* Knopf Doubleday Publishing Group.

Williams, C. (1974). *The destruction of Black civilization.* Third World Press.

Made in the USA
Las Vegas, NV
28 October 2023

79866651R00066